Winds From San Francisco: A Life Across Oceans

By

Duckhwan Kim

Copyright © 2024 by Duckhwan Kim

All rights reserved.
No portion of this book may be reproduced in any form without written permission from the publisher or author except as permitted by U.S. copyright law.

Disclaimer

No part of this publication may be reproduced, distributed, or transmitted in any form or by any means, including photocopying, recording, or other electronic or mechanical methods, without the prior written permission of the author, except in the case of brief quotations embodied in reviews and certain other non-commercial uses permitted by copyright law. Any unauthorized use of this material is strictly prohibited.

While every effort has been made to ensure the accuracy of the information contained within this publication, the author assumes no responsibility or liability for any errors or omissions. The information is provided "as is" without any warranties, either express or implied.

To My Beloved Sisters

Table of Contents

Chapter 1: Soaring Beyond Limits

- This Morning...
- Gunshots in a Quiet City
- Thirty Seconds of Happiness
- Good Neighbors in Hard Times
- My 'Burning Friday'
- My Lonely Prayer
- Farewell to 2016
- Reaching for the Sky

Chapter 2: Finding What Was Lost

- "Everyone, Gather Around!"
- Unforgettable Meeting In Silicon Valley
- Sammo's Song
- Postcards from San Francisco
- Squashing Competition
- " Yobosesyo~"
- A Sad Obituary
- Reflections on the Year's End

Chapter 3: Fighting On, Together

- "Fight On!"
- A Year Begins with Reconciliation
- Reuniting with My Son
- The Shanghai Twist
- My Apology to Victor
- Unchi Focus Lens
- "Ah, San Diego!"
- As Autumn Arrives

Chapter 4: The Dew on the Rose

- Jerry's Secret Diary
- 'Dew on That Rose...'
- "Hello, Amir!"
- The Red-crowned Crane
- Warm Soup and Jambalaya
- "Oh, My Toledo!"
- Make America Great Again
- Tora, Tora, Tora!!

Chapter 5: Precious Moments, Precious People

- To My Dear: The Sorrow Left Behind
- Reflections on My Vietnamese Friends
- Morning of Awakening
- Edelweiss
- Filled with Excitement Even at Dawn
- To My Beloved Sisters
- Cherishing Precious Moments and People
- Until the Sky Calls Us

Chapter 6: A Star Shining at Night

- The Poster at Kelowna
- Guests from the Rambla
- The Happy Sound
- On a Starry Starry Night
- Memories of Manila Grass Square
- Hello, Mr. Hargrove!
- The Owl of the Shoreline
- Only Sadness Remains

Chapter 7: A River Runs Through It

- Biden Takes Office Amid Conflict
- A River Runs Through It
- The Magnolia Falls, the Cherry Blossoms Bloom
- Cauliflower Love in May
- Erhua: The Boss of the Sick
- The Hydrangeas in Lombard Street
- I Miss You, Auntie
- The Flower of Blessings
- Love in Silicon Valley
- 3355 Torrance

Chapter 8: Half Moon Bay's Dobermannn

- Miss You Aunt
- Edelweiss in San Francisco
- Galaxy Express 999
- Oh, the Grand Canyon!
- The Dobermann of Half Moon Bay
- Nothing Lasts Forever
- Giants of Silicon Valley's Korean Community
- Vancouver... The Delay and Delight
- Reflections on Hangul Day

Chapter 9: Barefoot Isadora

- The Korean Chipmunk of Las Vegas
- A Rabbit in the Rain
- Barefoot Isadora
- A Defector's Legacy
- Happy Holidays in Chiang Mai!
- Sis, Boom, Bar~
- Dedicated to the 40th Anniversary of the 78th Air Force Academy
- Port Lee Arirang

Prologue

'Daffodils? No... What was this flower that bloomed so beautifully?'

It was five years ago, just before the pandemic in the spring of 2019. Time has passed swiftly since my elementary school days more than fifty years ago. Back then, Chaesik, the brightest girl in our class and the subject of envy for all the boys met me again in San Francisco through BAND. This was her first trip to the United States.

After settling her luggage at her uncle's house in Garden Grove, Southern California, where he had immigrated as a student and grown into a respected intellectual, she traveled to San Francisco with her older sister. The flowers hadn't yet bloomed, and the famed Lombard Street, with its winding, picturesque road, seemed nothing unusual. However, one Sunday, the hydrangeas in Lombard Street were in full bloom, a stunning display of vibrant colors.

The scene was too beautiful to enjoy alone, so I recorded a video as I slowly drove through the area, later uploading it to my elementary school classmates' BAND. Their reactions were as if they could see the beauty through my eyes, their cheers echoing as if in a shared dream.

"If you're going to San Francisco,

Be sure to wear some flowers in your hair.

If you're going to San Francisco,

You're gonna meet some gentle people there."

"For those who come to San Francisco,

Summertime will be a love-in there.

In the streets of San Francisco,

Gentle people with flowers in their hair."

Scott McKenzie's famous song was released in 1967, when I was just a young boy in second grade. San Francisco hummed to its tune, a city alive with promise and allure. I was an outsider, knowing little of the holy deeds of St. Francis, yet the name alone—San Francisco—had already become synonymous with desire, a place people from all over the world dream of visiting at least once in their lives.

It has now been 23 years since I left my homeland and made this beautiful bay area my home, far across the Pacific Ocean. When I first arrived, I never imagined I would stay this long in such an unfamiliar and strange place. As I look back on those 23 years of my life as an immigrant in San Francisco, I see a journey of hardship, with little time for leisure and constant battle to survive.

It was no surprise that I had to hastily board a sorrow-filled flight to Korea when my mother, whom I hadn't seen in years, passed away alone in a log cabin at the foot of Cheonhwangsan Mountain in Miryang.

Living the life of an immigrant, alone and without any guarantees from anyone, I faced countless trials and errors that were far from laughable. I often thought, *"If only I had someone to guide me, someone to show me the way with warmth and understanding."* Yet, as I sighed in regret, time had already carried me to a remote, countryside-quiet train station in life, a lonely place where the cosmos swayed in the breeze, untouched by the world.

What unexpectedly kept me going through the solitude and hardship of my immigrant life was my hobby of writing. I could not even measure the depth or literary quality of my own work, but the stories I had kept inside me for eight long years were written with sincerity and sent to the Korean Times in the Americas every month. To my surprise, these writings received a warm and gentle response from both the editorial desk and the readers, eventually leading to their compilation into a book. It was like an unexpected, cherished gift in a life that otherwise had nothing extraordinary to boast about.

With the publication of this book, what could bring me more joy than the chance to share, even in a small way, the joys, sorrows, and inspirations of the 7 million Korean compatriots who, like me, left the Joseon Peninsula, where for thousands of years they had carried their ancestors' legacies? These Koreans, scattered across the globe, are now writing the ongoing history of the Korean diaspora with their indomitable spirit, like resilient weeds that thrive wherever they take root. Through this book, I aim to reach those just beginning their own journey on this path.

Chapter 1

"Soar Beyond Limits: Dream High!"

This Morning...

Thursday, September 28, 2006

Summer already seems to be over. It slips away quietly, leaving behind just one vivid memory: a weekend in mid-July, when I found myself at a loss, wiping away the sweat that streamed down my body in the scorching 104-degree heat, something I had never experienced before.

Over the past four and a half years, since settling in the U.S., my American friends — whom I meet almost every morning at the YMCA in Palo Alto, a quiet city nestled in Silicon Valley — have been my companions. The YMCA offers excellent facilities, helping me jump-start my lonely and challenging immigrant life with renewed energy and a clean slate. Together, we lament the passing of summer, with my friends often remarking, "Summer's gone!" Their expressions reflect a shared regret for the fleeting season.

Each morning, I soak in the spa, letting the jets of water unknot the tension in my back. As I sit there, I find myself sighing, recalling the difficult times I've faced. Sometimes, I throw an imaginary uppercut into the water, as if fighting back against the struggles, determined to find new solutions. Whenever I meet

Scott — an American man in his 60s who has always been generous with his time and advice — we engage in long conversations, even if they are in my broken English. The YMCA has become a sanctuary, a precious place that offers me small moments of happiness and peace in my daily life.

When I first arrived in the U.S., I was filled with curiosity and wonder. I found myself asking questions like, *How do gyms here operate? How do people shower? How do they wrap their towels, and how do they navigate the pool?* Everything felt so unfamiliar, so new, and I approached it all with caution. The people I encountered each day looked different, and their skin tones were so diverse that it hit me: I was truly in America.

But now, after four and a half years, I think of everyone I know — whether they are white or Black — as my neighbors. These years have quietly helped me to assimilate, and I feel much more at home in this society.

As I cycle the three miles to the YMCA each morning, the cool Northern California breeze hits my body, greeting me as I ride along the familiar road. Just yesterday, on this same stretch, I passed a boy, perhaps a third-grader, who had fallen off his bike. His eyes were brimming with tears as he called home, and the sight tugged at me.

Further down the road, I noticed a squirrel, which usually darts across the street in a flash, pausing briefly to make onlookers' hearts race. But today, the squirrel walked with a slower, more deliberate gait, something large clasped in its mouth. I wondered if it was being greedy and should have just picked up an acorn. But as I turned to take a closer look, I saw the squirrel's silhouette outlined against the faint shadows still lingering on the road. For a moment, it appeared as if the squirrel were wearing a fox-fur scarf, or perhaps locked in a deep embrace with a partner, and I nearly laughed at the thought.

But then, as I watched the squirrel take a few heavy breaths and slowly climb the tree with its entire body, my heart ached.

The object the mother squirrel was holding was her baby, still gasping for breath. It had been slightly hit by a passing car while attempting to walk on the road for the first time and was slowly losing consciousness. The mother, in a desperate bid to save her injured child, gripped it gently in her mouth as she struggled to climb back up to the nest in the tree. The scene was heartbreaking, but it made me realize how trivial and limited my previous ideas about squirrels and other small creatures had been.

I used to think that these small animals, with their delicate bodies and fluffy tails, simply stood tall, looked around, and then quickly climbed up trees, unaware of deeper emotions. But seeing this pitiful sight today — the mother seemingly swallowing her tears, struggling to carry her injured baby up to the nest, 10 meters high in the tree — made me reconsider. For a fleeting moment, I wondered if they were once humans who had made some misstep in the afterlife, only to be reborn as seemingly insignificant creatures.

Living in America and watching children grow, I've often been disappointed when things didn't meet my expectations. But after witnessing the squirrels this morning, I find myself being more forgiving, learning to embrace them with greater understanding.

It was, without a doubt, a meaningful morning — one that led me to reflect on a valuable lesson: in life, we should never be cowardly or lose the spirit of determination, like the rising strength of Mount Baekdu. At the same time, I learned that we should not hastily judge others as insignificant. Instead, we should remain humble and respectful of everyone.

Gunshots In a Quiet City

2014-11-29 (Sat)

"No! ... My brother was such a good, family-oriented kid...."

As I opened the newspaper, my eyes widened in shock. I could still hear his sister's anguished cries, her grief spilling over as she mourned her brother.

In Menlo Park, a quiet city in Silicon Valley with a population of around 30,000, the silence was shattered by a dozen gunshots in broad daylight — an incident unlike anything the area had seen in years. The shocking event, which was still the talk of the town days later, had taken place on a street I drive past at least three or four times a week.

The suspect, a white man in his early 50s and known as a career office burglar, had been trying to escape from police after an employee reported suspicious activity. As he fled, he pulled out a gun and aimed it at the pursuing officers. In response, the police fired back, striking him in the face. He died at the scene. Reports indicated that three officers had opened fire, turning his final moments into a storm of bullets.

His sister's heart-wrenching cries were a poignant protest against the police department's official statement, which claimed they had no choice but to eliminate a dangerous criminal who had threatened their officers with a weapon.

What kind of life must a resident of Riverside County have led to end up here, attempting to break into an office, only to be shot 16 times and die?

After finishing my morning swim at the YMCA, I sit in the poolside jacuzzi and let my mind drift. The more I think about it, the more a chill runs down my spine.

Eleanor, a criminal defense attorney sitting beside me, shared her thoughts on the situation. She explained that while it was a grave mistake for the suspect to pull a gun out of desperation after being cornered, the police could have handled it differently. "If they had just fired one shot in a non-lethal area," she said, "the suspect would have surrendered and submitted to arrest right away. But instead, they concentrated their fire, creating unnecessary casualties. It was an abuse of power."

I cautiously asked if it was an inconvenient truth about American police — that they would rather shoot to kill than risk injuring someone with a poorly aimed shot. Eleanor reassured me that this was not the case.

The lawyer lady was aged looks like a grandmother. She frequently visits the criminal court and sometimes overhears police radio conversations. Once, an officer at the scene of a crime was given instructions by headquarters to shoot, but instead, he chose to de-escalate the situation. He talked the suspect down, convincing him to surrender without incident. "It's not always about pulling the trigger," Eleanor said.

Silicon Valley, known as the hub of cutting-edge technology, seems worlds apart from violence, but gun-related incidents do occur here from time to time. It's a reminder that if you act without caution, you could end up in serious trouble.

In Korea, the likelihood of a gun-related incident is minimal, but in many ways, the United States is a country where the enforcement of public power can be shockingly brutal.

If you react to a police officer's commands with anger or defiance, asking, "Is this how a democratic police force operates?" you may find yourself in grave danger. This is a country where absolute obedience to the police is often non-negotiable. It's not just a matter of following the rules; failing to comply can mean risking your life in a nation where the line between public order and brute force is sometimes razor-thin.

Thirty Seconds of Happiness

                                2015-06-27 (Sat)

Former Minister of Culture, Lee O-young, recently published a new book titled *A Goodnight Kiss to My Daughter*. In reading an interview with the author about the book, I sensed his deep regret and sorrow over his daughter, the late Pastor Lee Min-ah, who passed away three years ago after battling a chronic illness. The pain of love that went unshared between father and daughter permeates the pages, leaving a lasting impression.

Back in January 1978, just before graduating from high school, I visited a friend's house in Dangjin. I had been to Busan to pay my respects to my grandmother and was making my way back to Seoul. After a long, shaky ride on a local bus from Cheonan Station — nearly four hours of boredom — I finally arrived at my friend's rural home, where the faint sound of a chapel bell echoed from a nearby hill.

We wandered around the neighborhood, visited the elementary school my friend had attended, and ate Hotteok at the local market around noon. As we walked, we shared our youthful anxieties about the future, which loomed uncertainly but steadily approached us nonetheless.

Later that evening, after dinner, as our conversation dwindled, I noticed a book on the shelf. It was by Professor Lee O-young, a renowned intellectual at the time. I picked it up, lay down beneath the dim glow of fluorescent lights, and began turning the pages.

I don't exactly remember the title of the book, but it was a collection of essays about the new cultural trends that were popular among young people at the time, like beat rhythms and disco. I read it intently, thinking to myself, *"I need to read this to join the ranks of intellectuals."* However, as a young and immature person, I found the content difficult to grasp. I remember thinking, *"What a knowledgeable professor he must be."*

Now, this new book reflects on the former minister's deep regret over not spending enough time with his daughter because he was so consumed with writing the very books I had read in the quiet countryside of Chungcheong Province some 40 years ago. The book carries a heartbreaking message of remorse — the anguish of a father who considers himself cruel and incompetent, unable even to give his daughter a simple 30-second goodnight kiss during her childhood when she craved his attention the most.

I deeply relate to the part where he writes that life is a practice-free existence, and we all awkwardly navigate our roles. It's true. We live as awkward parents, awkward spouses, and awkward children, stumbling through life without a guide.

Steve Jobs, co-founder of Apple, was so busy living life on his own terms and changing the world that he passed away without ever meeting his biological father, who was of Syrian descent and lived in Sacramento — just a two-hour drive from Silicon Valley. In the U.S., you often hear the term "biological father/mother," a somewhat derogatory expression used to describe someone with whom you share only a biological connection but lack a deeper, emotional bond.

Even if his biological father had abandoned him, and even if he was "just" his biological father, shouldn't Jobs have met him at least once before he died? As a regular person, I can't help but inwardly chastise him.

Before death separates us forever, if there is someone you need to show respect, love, or seek reconciliation with, I hope you take the chance to do so. Why not pause for a moment, put aside whatever you're doing, and make that phone call?

Good Neighbors in Hard Times

2016-09-17 (Sat)

"Hey~" My mother's voice trailed off, weak and hesitant. "Go to Kyung-chul's house and get a sack of rice on credit." At that moment, a cold sweat ran down my face. "I've already explained everything to him, so he'll give it to you. Hurry."

In the early 1970s, two young brothers from the countryside opened a petroleum store in the neighboring town. Their business began with large jars of petroleum buried in the ground, allowing customers to scoop up what they needed. Before long, they started selling rice in a corner of the store. However, rice and petroleum made for an unfortunate combination to sell together.

Every time I lit the kerosene stove, I'd wince at the sharp, pungent smell. One day, when my mother went to buy kerosene, the store owner offered her rice at half price, claiming it had absorbed only a drop of kerosene. My mother, trying to make do, bought a bushel and cooked it. But the moment we tasted the rice, the overwhelming kerosene smell made it inedible.

With no food left and forced to throw away the pot of rice and what remained of the bushel, my mother, desperate and out of options, asked me to run the errand.

"Oh, come on! Kyung-chul is my classmate. How can I go to his house and ask for rice on credit? I just can't." I grumbled loudly, but I knew I couldn't disobey my mother. The thought of going to my friend's rice shop, imagining the possibility of being turned away, filled me with dread.

At home, we used old military duffel bags to store rice. I always felt a sense of comfort when the sacks were full, holding about two *mals* (a traditional grain measure that holds roughly 8 kilograms). But day by day, the bags would shrink, and when my mother scraped the bottom to gather the last grains, a heavy gloom would settle over me as if I were carrying all the worries of the world on my shoulders.

Our house was on a hill, and if you went down the road, there was a garbage dump on one side, and across the street stood Kyung-chul's rice shop. With my head hanging low and my voice barely more than a whisper, I approached Kyung-chul's father and explained my mother's request.

Without a word, Kyung-chul's father scooped a generous amount of rice from the mat and filled a round, one-*mal* bucket. He carefully scraped away the excess rice with a wooden spoon, stopping when it was level with the top.

When he placed the rice in a yellow paper bag and handed it to me, still without a word, the heavy weight of my worries suddenly lifted. I had felt so downcast, but in that moment, it was as if I had won the world. I walked home with light steps, breathing a deep sigh of relief.

Kyung-chul's house was the only rice shop in the neighborhood, and they were always kind to those who couldn't pay on time. They never frowned or showed any sign of displeasure when visited by those in need.

Instead, they treated everyone with warmth and kindness. Even now, whenever I think of that family, a warm smile spreads across my face.

Fifteen years ago, shortly after 9/11, I immigrated across the Pacific to work at a Korean bank in Northern California. Today, I work as a real estate and finance professional and have settled in Silicon Valley, the epicenter of the global information revolution. It is the wealthiest region in the United States, a world apart from the mountain village of my childhood back in Korea.

As part of my job, I occasionally step into mansions worth tens of millions of dollars, and sometimes even ultra-luxurious homes valued at $100 million. These are owned by global IT CEOs, executives, high-earning engineers, and venture capitalists — people whose wealth seems unimaginable compared to where I came from.

Back home, while people are much better off than they once were, there's still widespread discontent stemming from relative deprivation and the deep-rooted conflict between social classes. Here in Silicon Valley, despite the vast disparity between the rich and the poor, the neighborhood appears peaceful. On the surface, everyone seems content with their means, no matter how great the differences in wealth.

But sometimes I wonder. Do the wealthy of Silicon Valley — who live comfortably within their high walls — think about the underprivileged around them, those who struggle just as I did 40 years ago in my homeland? Do they offer warmth and care when help is needed, or are they disconnected from the hardships of others?

I find myself missing the 1970s in my home country, when even in difficult times, we shared warmth and compassion with our neighbors.

Thank God It's Friday!
TGIF

2016-10-22 (Sat)

Ding! My alarm chimed as it was time to go to the walk. I stop working and glance at my phone.

"Most Asians are too reserved!" commented Youngsu, who runs a small bakery café in Incheon. It was his response to the dance class video I had just posted.

"Right? I guess I was too shy to participate," I replied. Kind-hearted Youngsu is a comrade from the Pilseung (Certain Victory) Air Force, with whom I shared six months in the barracks at the Tanbang-dong training camp in Daejeon 33 years ago.

In Korea, Fridays are called *TGIF* or *Bulgeum* (literally meaning "Fire Friday"), and it's a day when everyone enjoys a drink and samgyeopsal (Pork Belly BBQ). Here in downtown Palo Alto, just in front of Stanford University, the vibe is different, but the weekend spirit remains the same. Friends and couples gather on restaurant patios, clinking glasses of wine, reflecting on the week, and sharing stories as the romantic atmosphere gradually warms up.

I'm at a community center, a little away from the

bustling downtown. On this Friday evening, around 100 students, men and women alike, have gathered for a ballroom dance class. They step briskly to the instructor's commands, his voice coming through a wireless microphone turned down low, out of respect for the neighbors. The instructor, as graceful as a swallow dipping into water, raises his hand and spins it twice. At this signal, the men move one space to the right, switching partners with each turn.

There are Korean students here, so I occasionally hear familiar conversations in Korean. Even though it's a social dance class, something that isn't embarrassing at all, I still feel awkward joining in with those who seem to be having so much fun. It's been 15 years since I came to the U.S. in search of a new world, yet nothing has really changed for me.

Even at the YMCA, which I visit every day, I stick to swimming and the jacuzzi. I've never played basketball or volleyball like many others do. The same goes for classes like Zumba — an intense aerobics class — or Tai Chi and yoga, which my Chinese friend Ray, who works at Oracle, volunteers to teach every Friday.

On *Friday nights*, when homesickness hits me hardest, I visit my best friend's house in Belmont and enjoy my sister-in-law's cooking. We have a nutritious meal filled with various grains, smoked salmon, sirloin barbecue, asparagus, and other dishes. We wash it all down with Corona beer, chatting and enjoying each other's company.

Or I might watch a touching movie like *Sully* about the 2009 flight that was in danger when a flock of birds struck its engines, but thanks to the captain and crew's quick thinking, they safely made an emergency landing, saving all 155 people on board. Sometimes, I'll sit by a quiet window at Starbucks, listening to music on my iPad as I browse Facebook leisurely. When I come across news of a volcanic eruption in Kyushu, Japan, I'll send a message to my friend who lives there, checking in and exchanging greetings.

I also slowly read novels like *To Kill a Mockingbird* over the course of a year, looking up unfamiliar words one by one on my smartphone using Google. Though I constantly search for the meanings of words and fill the margins of every page with notes, the novel doesn't flow through me effortlessly the way a Korean novel like Pak Kyongni's *Land* would.

Author Harper Lee provided immense inspiration to Americans with just two books in her lifetime, shedding light on the complexities of race relations between Black and white communities. *To Kill a Mockingbird* became a bestseller immediately after its publication in 1960 — the year I was born — and won the Pulitzer Prize the following year. Born in 1926, the same year as my mother, Lee lived alone in Monroeville, Alabama, until she passed away at the age of 90 in February, just as I was reading her second book, *Go Set a Watchman*.

Winning a Pulitzer Prize for a debut novel is a feat comparable to a major league rookie winning the batting triple crown and stolen base title in their first season. I cannot help but feel the utmost respect for Harper Lee, a great soul who brought such a powerful message and profound inspiration to society.

Now, I have a small plan for my Friday night: re-enroll in Netflix and watch the 1962 film adaptation of *To Kill a Mockingbird*, directed by Robert Mulligan and starring Gregory Peck, from the comfort of my own home.

My Lonely Prayers

2016-11-26 (Sat)

"You are the Answer to My Lonely Prayer."

I walk along the beach, listening to Neil Sedaka's *You Mean Everything to Me*, released over 40 years ago, playing through my earphones. "I've been sitting too long. It's time to take a walk," I think to myself, as I get a gentle but unignorable reminder from my smartphone app after being buried in work for over three hours.

Usually, after walking about 4 kilometers, my blood circulation improves, and on days when I walk after lunch and break into a light sweat, I feel pleasantly drowsy. I often indulge in a sweet, sluggish state for about 10 minutes, but when I wake up, I feel completely refreshed. What a wonderful world we live in — where the smartphone in your hand can guide you to a healthier lifestyle.

As I walk, I notice bluebirds perched on the bushes, long-billed sandpipers busily splashing in the shallow waters of the mudflats, and white-crowned cranes gazing intently at the water's edge. In the distance, far to the north of the mudflats, the skyscrapers of downtown San Francisco rise, 30 miles away, and I can see national airliners descending for landing at San Francisco Airport.

I can't thank Facebook enough for its incredible

technology that connects people all over the world and for providing such a fantastic trail to walk on. However, I can't shake the feeling that this luxury might last for only a month, and my heart feels as gloomy as the rainy season, with the sky pouring down like endless raindrops.

Global IT companies in Silicon Valley boast their vast, bustling campuses. Google in Mountain View is a prime example, and Apple in Cupertino is no exception. They're constructing a new 2.5 million-square-foot headquarters, which will resemble a flying saucer when seen from a satellite.

Facebook, which began in a cramped office in Palo Alto, has since moved into the massive Menlo Park campus previously occupied by Sun Microsystems, a company that collapsed during the dot-com crash more than a decade ago. Over time, Facebook has been steadily buying up business parks in the area, pushing out tenants one by one.

Despite being a global social networking giant with over 1 billion users, I can't quite fathom what they need all that office space for. To make matters worse, I've been told I have to move out of the building I currently live in because Facebook has asked everyone to vacate by the end of the year.

I have truly loved this office environment over the past five years, thanks to its convenient location and excellent facilities, including state-of-the-art conference rooms. Sometimes, I feel frustrated with Facebook for forcing this change, but then I remember Mark Zuckerberg's remarkable gesture of donating 98% of his stock to society, and my heart melted over that generous act.

Every company I interact with asks me, "Are you staying with us, or have you looked elsewhere?" They show concern about my situation, and it's disheartening to face the prospect of being forced to relocate. As I reflect on the year, which seems to have passed by unusually quickly, I find myself grappling with the dilemma of moving my office. This time of year feels both exciting and solemn, and even someone as indecisive as I am has to make a choice by December.

Despite the challenges I've faced in business this year, I've been reflecting on what I'm genuinely thankful for. It hasn't been an easy year, but when I take a moment to think deeply, I realize there are still things for which I can be grateful.

At the beginning of the new year, shortly after returning from Korea, I went for a long-distance run over the weekend but had to stop frequently, gasping for breath. Concerned, I got a blood test, and the results showed that my shortness of breath was caused by low hemoglobin and anemia. Since anemia is a warning sign for people over 50, I quickly scheduled a gastrointestinal endoscopy, a mid-abdominal MRI, and a venous thrombosis test. The doctors explained that in our age group, blood deficiencies could sometimes be linked to internal bleeding caused by stomach or colon cancer, so it was crucial to investigate further.

During the two days, I waited for the results, I mentally prepared myself, imagining countless outcomes with a sense of urgency that felt even stronger than waiting for college entrance exam results. *If it's cancer, I should do this...* and so on.

When the news finally came, it was a relief: nothing was wrong. The happy prescription was simply to take iron supplements for three months and focus on improving my diet with more vegetables. I don't think there's anything I'm more thankful for this year. Money comes and goes, and a business slump? It's not worth worrying about in comparison.

Now, the only thing left is to find a new office. I wonder

what kind of wonderful space God will provide as an answer to my lonely prayer.

Farewell to 2016

2016-12-31 (Sat)

Drip, drip, drip... I wake up at dawn to the sound of heavy winter rain. After savoring a brief moment of sweet laziness, I quickly get dressed and head out to work. The winter drought that has plagued California for the past four years and caused severe water shortages seems to be easing. The ground is damp, but many businesses remain closed, and the freeway is eerily empty.

While many people spend their days lounging under palm trees, sipping cocktails in the sun, it's also peaceful to quietly reflect on the year in the solitude of an empty office. This is how the year comes to an end.

I first began to understand the concept of years when I entered middle school and encountered the textbook *1972 Complete Conquest of Mathematics*. The passage of time began to settle in my mind. The following year, as I entered the second grade, the new textbook was titled *1973 Complete Conquest of Physical Sciences*. Since then, 44 years have passed, and now, no matter how much I might resist, I must lay 2016 to rest in my memory.

2016 was a year marked by separation.

I decided to step down from my volunteer work assisting

seniors in the industry. For a significant period of four years, I served as the education director for the Korean Association of Real Estate & Lending Professionals, organizing various seminars and contributing to the drafting and publication of the industry's professional charter.

What would happen to the market if fellow professionals competed fiercely, each relying on exaggerated advertising? What I particularly remember is that we were able to present a fair path without resorting to such tactics.

I hope this new year will be one where common sense prevails and more people agree that it's wrong to disappoint colleagues by acting independently and disregarding the charter we worked so hard to establish.

Looking back, I don't think volunteering for the association's work caused any major disruptions to my business. However, I feel that after serving with joy for a sufficient amount of time, it's time to step aside. I left quietly, without saying a word.

There were also some meaningful encounters in 2016.

I met a friend at the Costco in Redwood City, which is about halfway between where we both live. We grabbed a quick lunch of freshly baked chicken bakes from the food court and caught up on various things. My friend's wife had thoughtfully packed five warm, home-baked sweet potatoes in a plastic bag, telling me to heat them up and eat them whenever I felt hungry. It was such a simple yet heartfelt gift.

We are BFFs — best friends forever — always there for each other whenever needed. How comforting it is to have a friend like this in my new immigrant life. While pushing a cart and chatting about this and that, I ran into Sam, a big name in the same industry, whom I hadn't seen in a long time. Sam is from Lebanon, and he's my age, yet he dominates the commercial real estate market in downtown Palo Alto — the most coveted location in Northern California.

What I've learned from Sam, who has been in the business far longer than I have, is the power of perseverance. He has a slight disability in his legs and can't walk quickly, but he never loses his composure or becomes discouraged. He negotiates with calmness and precision, never letting his guard down until the deal is done. I deeply admire the strength and patience it must have taken for him, a Middle Eastern immigrant, to build and maintain such a stellar reputation in Silicon Valley — an environment teeming with fierce competitors.

2016 was also a year when friends from abroad came to visit me. Who are the immigrants leading the way in American hotels, gas stations, and IT companies in Silicon Valley? They are the Indians. An Indian hotelier who owns several hotels across Silicon Valley and throughout California recently reached out to me to become friends. It's incredible to share business insights and help one another achieve our big dreams.

A few days ago, a Jewish businessman who runs a successful brunch restaurant in Oakland, Ca contacted me. He had seen my name on the Business Marketplace website and felt that we could become good friends. How delightful.

I welcome the dawn of 2017 with excitement, carrying the promising energy of these new connections into my New Year's wishes.

Reaching for the Sky

2017-02-04 (Sat)

"America is a great country. Defending this country is a wonderful way to live. You can be a part of the United States Air Force. Dream big. Set your dreams high in the sky!"

Boom! This video, which ends with an exhilarating scene of a cutting-edge fighter jet soaring through the sky, is a U.S. Air Force recruiting ad. In 1983, I served diligently as a new second lieutenant at Wing Command on Osan Air Base, the key U.S. Air Force base in Korea. On Fridays, I would drink unfamiliar beers like Michelob and play games like pocket ball or hand darts with my classmates and U.S. Air Force counterparts at the officers' club. When the mood got lively, we'd head next door to the base theater to watch a movie like *Flashdance*. Before the movie began, my heart would race as I watched supersonic fighter jets perform acrobatic maneuvers in the sky, accompanied by the loud roar and the iconic last line: *"Aim High!"*

Yes, we should dream big... But now is not the time for me to pursue new dreams; it's a time to reflect on how many of my dreams have come true. If I ask myself whether I've achieved anything truly great in my life, the answer doesn't come easily.

If I had to choose a safe but truly significant

"achievement," it would be that my children have grown up well and are now able to take care of themselves. When I immigrated to the U.S. in 2002 with an H1-B work visa to serve the Korean community, my two sons were in the second grade of middle school and the fifth grade of elementary school. After barely adjusting to American school following one semester in Cerritos, Southern California, they had to transfer again when I moved to a new post in Silicon Valley, Northern California.

Helping my sons with their American school homework was beyond my abilities. Yet, miraculously, they managed to follow along in their English classes, complete their homework, and thrive in their new environment. I am so proud and deeply grateful for how well they've turned out. To ask for anything more would feel excessive.

Bob, who has sat across from me at the desk for years, recently gave me an old statistics book published in 1956 as a souvenir. He's four years older than me and is what you'd call a "Stanford kid." His father was a professor at the university, so he grew up in the campus's professor village. He lived away from Stanford only for four years while attending Princeton but returned to Stanford for his master's degree in computer science. He's now lived on the Stanford campus for nearly 45 years.

Recently, Bob's father passed away at the age of 98, and he took some time away from the office to attend the funeral. He told me he couldn't even begin to think about cleaning out his father's faculty office, where his father had served as a professor of statistics and economics. My curiosity was piqued, so I decided to accompany him.

The office was filled with books that had absorbed the breath of the great scholar for many years. As Bob climbed a ladder to organize the books and materials that filled the study, I asked if I could keep one of the books as a memento. He readily agreed and handed me one of his father's books as a gift.

I don't know what people who don't believe in the afterlife might think, but I told Bob that in my next life, I want to become a scholar. I want to be like his father — a world-renowned scholar, someone who contributes to humanity. Bob, ever the kind American, gave me a gentle smile and said he hoped that would happen.

When I reflect on my life, I see it as a series of days spent worrying about the reality in front of me. Why did dreaming big always seem so far away, as though I was trapped within the confines of my immediate circumstances?

After struggling to graduate from college and serving in the Air Force for 42 months to fulfill my national defense duty, I, like most of my peers, entered the workforce as a salaryman once I was discharged. The weight of reality felt too heavy to pursue my dream of continuing my studies for a master's or doctorate degree, especially with the prospect of studying abroad. I found myself confined, thinking that the obstacles before me were too great to overcome.

If I had received a strong enough pushback then and dared to push my limits by pursuing further studies abroad, would my life now be different? If I had the chance to go back in time and speak to my younger self, I would urge him not to be confined by the challenges in front of him but to dream big and chase those dreams without hesitation. There's one message I would want to deliver most:

"Duckhwan put your dreams in the sky. Aim High!"

Chapter 2
Finding What Was Lost

"Everyone, Gather Around!"

2017-03-11 (Sat)

"I love you, Park Bo-gum!" Phoebe, Richard's Taiwanese wife, exclaimed with excitement. She was referring to Park Bo-gum, the lead actor in the Korean drama *Love in the Moonlight,* which aired last year.
"I've lost count of how many times I've watched it. It's just so good! I'm completely hooked!" she added, her voice brimming with enthusiasm.

Today, I met with my friends from Aqua Boot Camp, a water training class held every Saturday morning at the Palo Alto YMCA pool. We've been training together for anywhere from one to ten years. Fifteen of us, including our swimming companions and their families, had invited Maddie, our instructor—a young white woman in her mid-20s—to join us for a friendly lunch at a cozy Korean restaurant.

Richard, who was born in Vietnam and is of Chinese descent, is a family man through and through. With a hint of pride, he often says he likes to stop by Costco or the supermarket after class every Saturday to buy groceries and cook. He had been absent the previous week, which made me wonder what had happened. When he arrived at the restaurant today, he held up his left hand, showing off a bandaged ring finger. "I cut myself while cooking," he explained.

Richard never bothers his wife when she's deep into watching her beloved Korean dramas, and he always makes her delicious meals. It's no myth that Chinese men are great cooks—and their wives love them for it!

He immigrated to Paris with his parents during the Vietnam War. After serving in the French Army and graduating from college, he went to UPenn to study computer science, earned a master's degree, and settled in Silicon Valley. When he was laid off from Nokia 10 years ago, we shared a sense of empathy (if you haven't been laid off in the US, don't talk about life). He is now an executive at a company that provides online magazine subscription services.

The Taiwanese couple sitting next to him, Zer-Kang and Mei, are bioengineers who met as a teaching assistant and students in college, fell in love, and came to Indiana to study and earn their doctorates together. Unlike Mei, who has a gentle appearance, her husband Zer-Kang is the oldest among the men. Still, he boasts of his iron stamina, doing 30 push-ups after class, not satisfied with just doing all the events such as butterfly and individual medley without getting tired. According to a friend, he is an intellectual macho who gives off a bandit vibe.

Chris, in his late 40s, sitting across from me, is a central figure in an IT company in Silicon Valley and is handsome like a movie star of Chinese, Hawaiian, and European descent. He is the protagonist of a sweet love story with his Indonesian wife, Sarah, who met him when he bought books while working part-time at a bookstore in a junior college, and they ended up getting married.

Hisae, a Japanese woman in her late 60s, sat between Susan, a piano teacher from Shanghai, and Susan's quiet husband, Joseph. Hisae, originally from Tokyo and the daughter of a bathhouse owner, settled here after her husband retired from working at a Japanese tech company, RICO's Silicon Valley branch.

Susan shared that in her early 20s, she lived through the infamous Cultural Revolution, when Chairman Mao Zedong sent intellectuals to forced labor camps in the countryside, claiming he would establish a true communist system. This period, which began in 1966 and lasted about 10 years, filled her with despair. She recalled the bizarre rumors circulating at the time, like how Mao planned to use the best medical technology to help people live to be 150 years old.

As the room I booked became oversubscribed, Aida, an Ecuadorian MIT graduate, ended up sitting in the hallway with her Spanish husband, a college friend, and their two young children.

I felt a deep sense of camaraderie with all my friends, who had shown such sincerity by attending and treasuring this gathering. I handed out pairs of high-quality hiking socks—gifts from a friend in Korea—and seeing them smile from ear to ear brought me real joy.

It's incredible how we all came from different corners of the world yet came together to swim and bond. As we shared delicious Korean food and conversation, the chorus of the 1978 Village People song played in my mind:

Young man, there's no need to feel down.

I said, young man, pick yourself off the ground.

I said, young man, 'cause you're in a new town

There's no need to be unhappy.

It's fun to stay at the Y.M.C.A.

Unforgettable Meeting In Silicon Valley

2017-04-22 (Sat)

"Look at that deer!" She exclaimed while hiking the Stanford Dish Trail, named after the large satellite dish perched on the hill. A medium-sized blonde woman, who had been alternating between walking ahead and behind me along the four-mile trail, gestured toward a shaded area. When I looked closely, about a hundred meters away, I saw a doe standing apart from the herd, gazing off into the distance.

I was already feeling uneasy, and my mouth was dry from nervousness. Since I wasn't feeling up to my usual 20km Sunday morning run, I decided to go for a walk around the hill behind campus instead. It was a bit chilly, but I couldn't bear the thought of spending the day cooped up at home or in a coffee shop. So, I gathered my strength, walked for a while, and about a mile in, I struck up a conversation with Karen, who was on a business trip from New York to Silicon Valley.

When I complimented her, saying, "You have sharp eyes!" she laughed and told me she often hears people say she has "eagle eyes," able to notice the smallest details. She then showed me a photo on her phone of an unknown red wildflower, similar to a cosmos, that she had snapped by the roadside earlier.

We quickly became friends when I showed her a photo of a timid mole, its head barely poking out of the ground as it pushed moist dirt around its hole. She told me she worked in New York at the Nasdaq stock exchange and had taken this walk before heading back after a business trip to Silicon Valley, where she had met with corporate clients.

While her primary job involves discovering new companies to list, I wondered if marketing was also necessary for already-listed companies. She explained that part of her role is to ensure these companies experience no difficulties in raising capital by improving stock trading convenience. This way, they aren't tempted to switch to other markets, like the New York Stock Exchange.

She shared that she was born in Canada and spent seven years in Hong Kong with her father, who worked in international business. She'd even visited Korea at some point. Though she once lived in Silicon Valley, 20 years ago, she was selected by Nasdaq and has been settled in the West Central Park area of New York ever since. Recently, she gave up his Canadian citizenship to become a U.S. citizen. As she described her busy life overseeing marketing for 12,000 clients, including 3,000 Nasdaq-listed companies, she exuded the confidence of someone delighted with their career.

When I asked if she had any Korean corporate clients, she mentioned that none were directly under her management, but she was sure some of her colleagues handled companies from Korea.

She also mentioned her interest in collecting art and, with only two hours left before her flight to New York, hurried off to visit the De Young Museum, a prominent modern art museum in San Francisco. Her ability to plan her time so meticulously and live without any idle moments was truly inspiring to me.

In Buddhism, I've heard that a good friend who supports you and walks alongside you on the same path in life is called a *doban*. It's a beautiful concept to live with the hope of meeting your doban and imagining when such a friend might come into your life. However, it's important not to waste precious time searching for the "perfect" *doban*. Only when you accept that you are not perfect yourself can you overlook the flaws in others. If you're fortunate enough to find a *doban* with whom you can share your deepest thoughts without shame and walk the difficult road of life together, you can live gracefully, keeping your composure and smile—even when life feels heavy.

As we go through life, we sometimes drift apart from friends we thought would be by our side forever, and yet, at unexpected crossroads, we meet wonderful new friends.

Today was one of those special days. Walking through the final days of winter in San Francisco, with the lingering chill in the air, I found myself enjoying a brief but meaningful 30-minute conversation with good friends under the clear, blue sky.

"Sammo Song: A Tribute to Mom (who is in heaven)"

2017-05-27 (Sat)

Fifteen years ago, my mother and I drove along the FWY 5—a nearly 170-mile stretch of open plains—until we reached Bakersfield and the mountain road leading to LA. It felt special to be on a road trip with her for the first time in a long while, though I had no idea that this would be the road where we would part forever. During the long drive, I kept chatting with her about everyday matters—household chores, stories of my two grandchildren adjusting to school in the United States, and updates about my work.

At the time, I worked as a branch manager for a commercial bank located inside the headquarters of a large corporation, Daewoo, that pursued global management under the founder's catch praise. I often told myself, "Every Street Is Paved With Gold." I had recently settled in Silicon Valley after being hired by a Korean bank in California. My mother, eager to see how her third son was living in the U.S., had been encouraged to visit by my older brother, who arranged the trip for her.

My mother had built a log cabin at the foot of Cheonhwangsan Mountain, where the thousand-year-old Pyochungsa Temple, founded by Grand Master

Wonhyo of ancient Korea's Silla Dynasty, and where Samyeong Daesa practiced asceticism, still stands. For nearly 10 years, starting in my early 30s, I made the 15-hour drive to that remote yet beautiful mountain village every holiday to visit her. Those trips home remain some of my most cherished memories.

My mother lived alone in a mountain village, which left her feeling lonely. She had a white Jindo dog named Sooni, whom she loved dearly. Worried that Sooni (as of Jan 26, 2025) might go hungry during her trip to the U.S., she had asked the old man next door to feed her every morning and evening. But not long after my mother arrived in the U.S., news came that the old man, who had been drinking heavily, was bitten on the hand while feeding Sooni and had been hospitalized. This happened less than ten days after my mother arrived.

Since there wasn't much for her to do in my area—no familiar faces to socialize with and barely any public transportation—I couldn't leave her at home all day. Instead, I would drop her off at the senior center for Koreans in Santa Clara on my way to work and pick her up after. My mother, who loved being around people, immediately enjoyed herself with the other grandmothers and quickly became the star of the Hwatu: Korean cards game, impressing everyone with her skills. She even became the most popular among them, as she generously gave away nearly all her winnings as snacks for the others.

I never expected that the precious time I spent driving her to and from work would end so abruptly and in vain...

When my mother heard that our neighbor's grandfather had been hospitalized, she rushed back to Korea. Since her flight from San Francisco left early in the morning, we had to make the long drive across the vast California plains to LAX, where her night flight awaited.

It was four years later, since my mom returned to Korea, that I had a phone call one day from an immediate older sister to notify me of the mom's sudden demise. Until then, I had never been able to visit Korea because I was building a life in the United States. It came as such a big shock to me that I hurriedly caught a plane to Korea for the first time in 7 years since immigration.

Spring has passed, and now summer is beginning. I had always been so healthy that I thought I'd never get sick, but after a day of exposure to the cold wind due to a broken car window, I came down with the flu. For ten days, I alternated between daytime and nighttime medicine every four hours, battling through it.

Finally, after exactly ten days, the flu started to fade. One dawn, while drenched in sweat and tears, coughing and longing for my mother's comforting hands, she came to me in a dream for the first time in ten years. She gave me a warm kiss on the cheek and gently patted my back.

"Cheer up; everything will be okay," she whispered.

Soon after, my flu completely disappeared, and I began to see some signs of improvement at work.

May—the month when we celebrate our parents—is quietly slipping away.

"The persimmons placed on the plate are so lovely.

Though not Yuja(柚子|Yuzu), they are worth carrying home.

Yet, if I bring them back, there will be no one to delight in them,

and that makes me sad."

- Park Il-Ro (1561–1642), Joseon Dynasty

This line comes from a sorrowful poem about parents by Park, Il-Ro, a lyric poet from the mid-Joseon period. Friends, cherish and serve your parents while they are still with you.

Postcards from San Francisco

2017-07-01 (Sat)

I spent last Sunday in San Francisco, a city I hadn't visited in a while due to my busy schedule. I parked at the Presidio, once the U.S. Navy's headquarters during the Pacific War, and jogged across the Golden Gate Bridge. I planned to visit Sausalito, a beautiful tourist spot known for its galleries and cozy restaurants, and then take the ferry back.

A rare spectacle had occurred just a few days earlier—a humpback whale weighing over 30 tons swam beneath the Golden Gate Bridge with its calf. It was still lingering in the bay. Cargo ships slowly drifted toward the Pacific Ocean while yachts with white sails and colorful kayaks glided past, creating splashes that mirrored the playful movements of the water birds. The species has disappeared somewhere, no more around the Golden Gate Bridge.

As I gazed across the bay from Marin County, with the gleaming skyscrapers of downtown San Francisco in the distance, I was swept away by memories from 40 years ago.

My fourth uncle, an engineer on a merchant ship, traveled the world and would send postcards from the places he visited. One postcard to my father began with the words, "Dear Respected Elder Brother, I am sending you a letter." It featured a night view of the Golden Gate Bridge.

One day, I heard the exciting news that my uncle, who had spent a long year at sea, had finally arrived at Incheon Port. My aunt, heartbroken by their separation early in their marriage, had come up from Busan a few days prior and was eagerly counting down the days until we could all reunite.

It was a thrilling day, about 40 years ago, when my uncle arrived at our house in Donam-dong, where his eldest brother, my dad—who had struggled after a failed business—was living. My uncle arrived, dragging a large trunk full of mysterious items. He missed us dearly, especially my older sister, who was in middle school, and I, then in fifth grade, had another level of excitement. We were thrilled not only to see our beloved uncle but also to anticipate the treasures that might be hidden inside that trunk of gifts.

When my uncle patted my head and asked how I was doing, my elder sister and I were already fixated on the trunk. As he unzipped it with a grand swivel, we stared in awe, our eyes gleaming with excitement, certain that it would soon overflow with all kinds of treasures.

Finally, the trunk opened. My uncle handed my father, his eldest brother, a bottle of Johnnie Walker whiskey—expensive and wrapped in a fancy shopping bag. For my mother, who was his sister-in-law, he presented a beautiful hand mirror that clicked open, along with Lancôme foundation and a red lipstick that carried a subtle fragrance.

For us, there were Parker fountain pens, which were incredibly popular at the time, small Hershey's chocolates wrapped in triangular foil with stoppers, and even a delicious orange—something we had only ever seen in picture books.

We were overjoyed for days as if we had won the world. Each of my five uncles had a unique personality that shaped our childhood memories, but this uncle was particularly special. Before getting married, he worked as a police officer in Mapo and was a constant source of support during my older sister's and my sensitive teenage years. Even though his salary was modest, when he as struggling to pay for boarding and living expenses, he never failed to come by on payday with an envelope for his sister-in-law to help with household costs. He was always looking out for his brother, doing everything he could, and served as a steady emotional pillar for us.

My uncle met my beautiful aunt through a matchmaker. She graduated from a local prominent Jinju Girls' High School, and they married later in life in Busan. I would like to mention that my uncle was a relatively older bachelor to marry later than usual, but aunt was not that late. Using his college degree, he became an overseas sailor, determined to secure stability for his family, even if it meant enduring long periods away from home. His voyages took a year for each departure, but eventually, he established a solid foundation for himself and his family.

However, as my aunt's tuberculosis worsened, my uncle couldn't bear to leave her behind any longer. He decided to step off the overseas ship for good and never sailed again.

My aunt, who had blessed me with a lovely cousin at a time when I longed for a younger sister, passed away just a few months later. Although the doctors and those around her advised her to go to a nursing home for intensive care, she hesitated. She couldn't be able to leave such lovely and precious children behind and, unfortunately, missed the chance for proper treatment.

My dear, affectionate uncle became a single man and lived alone for 40 years, only becoming a grandfather in his early 80s. Who can stop the passage of time? It saddens his brother deeply to know that only two of my five uncles remain and that the generation of uncles in our family is slowly coming to an end.

I remembered my dear, respected uncle with a sense of longing, hoping that his later years would be filled with more happiness. I wish I could write and send a postcard from San Francisco, the very place my uncle sent my dad a postcard from some 40 years ago.

Friendship Squash

2017-08-12 (Sat)

We came out of the pool, panting, and headed straight for the jacuzzi, exchanging high-fives. I had hesitated to attend the underwater survival class, but after completing the one-hour training, I felt a sense of pride and relief that we had endured it together until the end. I couldn't help but smile broadly.

It's no small feat to swim for 20 minutes every day before work and then spend nearly an hour training in the water on Saturdays, almost like a naval recruit. Today, eight of us participated and safely completed the session.

Swimming is truly an excellent exercise, and the benefits are countless. First, it helps with weight management: 30 minutes of breaststroke burns 367 calories, which is more than walking, cycling, or even running. Second, it reduces stress and enhances self-awareness. Third, it boosts your mood.

Fourth, it strengthens your muscles. Water offers 44 times more resistance than air, so naturally, you use much more muscle power. Fifth, swimming is a low-impact exercise. Thanks to the water's buoyancy, you only feel about 10% of your actual body weight, making it ideal for rehabilitation after surgery or intense exercise.

Sixth, it promotes better sleep. Since swimming demands significant physical effort, studies show that swimmers are twice as likely to enjoy a good night's rest compared to those who engage in other exercises. Seventh, it's a refreshing workout—no sweating, as the cool water absorbs your body heat. Lastly, swimming is great for cardiovascular health. It helps maintain a healthy heartbeat, lowers blood sugar and blood pressure, and reduces bad cholesterol. Regular swimming significantly lowers the risk of diabetes, heart disease, and stroke—an exercise you could continue until you're 100 years old!

Richard, our Chinese team leader, who swims as fast as a dolphin, quietly told me he'd meet me in the hall after our showers. He brought a squash from his garden, a long, dark green one with a light-yellow base where the sun hadn't touched it. "How beautiful," I thought.

There are so many kinds of squash in the United States, each with different names. Zucchinis are long like cucumbers; there's a squash with a blunt base resembling two gourds stacked together and pumpkins—famous for their weight contests in the fall. In Northern California, the Half Moon Bay Pumpkin Weigh-Off is well known. Last year, a giant pumpkin from Illinois weighed in at 2,145 pounds, the largest in North America and the second heaviest in the world. The record, set in Germany in 2014, is a staggering 2,323 pounds, equivalent to 12 heavyweight boxers!

Richard, my swimming buddy of 15 years, grew up in France after spending his early childhood in Vietnam. Though he's Chinese, we met here after traveling halfway across the world. Just like last year, he brought me the squash wrapped in a bag of Paris Baguette, a Korean franchise of bakery café at downtown Palo Alto.

Curious about how Koreans cook squash, he asked. I told him we often chop it up and add it to kimchi stew or soybean paste stew. He wanted to give it a try. Richard, who enjoys cooking, melted butter in a heated pan, sautéed onions until they softened, then added the squash. He stir-fried it over medium heat, lightly seasoning it with salt and pepper, and it turned out delicious.

As we sipped coffee afterward, Richard joked that it felt like yesterday when his older son started at Stanford and now he's a senior. Next month, he'll send his younger son to Washington University in St. Louis, and he's already worrying about the tuition when I said 'No worries' as his Palo Alto, Silicon Valley's premier residential house, increased value by $200,000 yearly, he just nodded with relief.

What is the connection between St. Louis and Washington? The university was founded in 1853 and named after the first U.S. president, George Washington. It's a prestigious private institution that ranks 19th among U.S. universities and has produced 25 Nobel Prize winners.

After sharing the squash he had lovingly grown and talking about life, we left the gym refreshed and a little tired from our swim but with bright expressions on our faces.

"Yoboseyo~"

2017-09-30 (Sat)

"**Yoboseyo~**" Everyone's eyes turned toward me. Joe, who always greets me warmly in Korean whenever we make eye contact in the locker room, is a 60-year-old American with a sturdy build, almost like a German soldier. He's Italian American and the vice president of Cisco Systems, one of the largest tech companies in Silicon Valley. Joe has a special affection for Korea, having frequently traveled on business to the Korean branch when he was younger, where he formed close relationships with the employees. However, the only Korean phrase he knows is "Yoboseyo~," which he learned from how the employees answered phone calls.

These days, the hottest topic at the gym is definitely North Korea's "Rocket Man," Kim Jong-un. When Joe asked, "He was quiet yesterday?" I smirked and replied, "Yeah, I told him not to shoot. Sometimes he listens to me," and the people around us burst into laughter.

It's not that things haven't been tense, but there's been a lull these past few days. Trump and Kim Jong-un have been exchanging fierce words, and the Korean Peninsula is in a state of crisis as U.S. strategic bombers fly closer to North Korean airspace to demonstrate military strength. Yet, there hasn't been any news of additional missile provocations.

Even though I share the same last name as Kim Jong-un, I know I'm unlikely to be even a distant relative, but my American friends at the Palo Alto YMCA still ask me all kinds of questions. Having been a member here for 15 years, I exercise, swim, and go to the sauna every morning, which has allowed me to make many friends. I've become relatively well-known as "the Korean guy" at the Palo Alto YMCA. But these days, with North Korea's reckless nuclear tests and missile launches, I've found myself drawing even more attention than usual.

"What should we do?" my friends ask me, their faces filled with concern. With a confident expression, I tell them that the more President Trump uses extreme phrases like "fire and fury" and "destruction," the more credibility he loses. I add that we must either take immediate military action or stop and find another solution. They listen closely, hanging on my words.

If President Clinton had taken decisive action during the first North Korean nuclear crisis in 1994, under South Korean President Kim Young-sam, we wouldn't be in the panic we find ourselves in now. But history doesn't allow for "ifs." Even today, there is still hope—we could see the best path forward by securing China's cooperation.

Twenty-three years ago, China was just starting to act as a subcontractor for advanced countries, offering cheap labor and getting its first real taste of global trade. In 1997, when I was working at a commercial bank in S. Korea and went on a business trip to Shanghai's Pudong District for a conference, there was only one tall structure—the Oriental Pearl TV Tower—standing alone in the middle of an empty field.

Back then, China wasn't a military threat to the U.S. and wasn't involved in all global affairs. Resolving the North Korean nuclear issue would have been far easier. But looking back, it seems the U.S. merely bought time. China has now transformed into a G2 power, with a foreign exchange reserve of $3.7 trillion, at least $2.5 trillion of which is from its trade surplus with the U.S. Rather than being grateful to the U.S. for this economic rise, China is flexing its muscles—building artificial islands in the South China Sea, challenging its neighbors, and being passive in sanctioning North Korea despite its violations of UN resolutions with nuclear tests and missile provocations.

China applies an entirely different standard to South Korea. Even though it knows that THAAD (Terminal High Altitude Area Defense) is a necessary defense system against North Korea's missile threats and is now aimed at China, it continues to make absurd claims and threats. There are reckless remarks like, "Eating kimchi has made them stupid," and even talk of bombing South Korea in response to THAAD's deployment. China has also encouraged a widespread boycott of South Korean companies operating in China. This behavior tarnishes China's reputation as a reliable international economic partner and further escalates tension on the Korean Peninsula.

At a time when gratitude should be ripening with the approach of Chuseok, South Korea finds itself caught in a turbulent wave of fear over North Korea's unpredictable nuclear missiles. My heart is heavy with worry for the family and friends I left behind. I sincerely hope this situation will resolve peacefully, that we can move toward reunification, and that good news will soon blow across the Pacific Ocean.

A Sad Obituary

2017-10-28 (Sat)

After enjoying a packed lunch I'd prepared at home, I head out for a lunchtime walk. It's been 10 months since I moved to the other side of the freeway after Facebook bought out the entire business park where my office used to be with its enormous cash flow.

When I first moved in last January, it was the rainy season, and the stream next to the building was deep and fast-moving, reminding me of the Uicheon River in Ui-dong, Seoul Seoul, where I lived my honeymoon days in the late 80s during the rainy season. Now, as I walk through the charming residential area along the valley, the once-powerful stream has dried up, leaving the riverbed exposed. My lunchtime walk takes me across the railroad tracks on a 3-mile round trip to the Nordstrom Department Store, located deep inside the Stanford Shopping Center. This walk brings me both joy and health.

As I cross the tracks, I notice a new job in Silicon Valley—a "track guard." This role was created after more than a dozen graduates and alumni from Palo Alto's Gunn High School, one of the most prestigious public schools, tragically took their own lives on the tracks in recent years. The school district negotiated with the city to hire track guards in an effort to prevent more tragedies.

The track guards closely monitor anyone who approaches the tracks for reasons other than simply crossing. Since they were put in place, I've noticed that such tragedies have decreased significantly. However, I recently heard the sad news of another accident in a nearby city.

I read the obituary carefully, written in elegant language that conveyed the family's deep sorrow with quiet grace. In the upper right corner, a photo of a smiling, pretty blonde girl caught my attention. The girl, Holly, was someone I never knew, as I don't have a daughter myself.

"Philip and Julie Spalletta's precious 14-year-old daughter, Holly, suddenly passed away on the 26th. Holly was a proud graduate of her beautiful neighborhood's elementary and middle school and a freshman at Sequoia High School, where she had deep friendships with her classmates.
She volunteered for the Society for the Prevention of Cruelty to Animals, was a member of the 4-H Club, and had just begun training to become a counselor for the club. Holly was a beautiful, kind, gentle, witty, and incredibly trustworthy daughter. She was a cherished friend to many, and the world was a more attractive place with her warm and caring spirit. If you knew her well, you'd be amazed.

"Holly leaves behind four older siblings, her parents, grandparents, uncles, cousins, and countless friends who cherished her. She had recently been gifted a BMW Mini Coupe in celebration of her starting high school, a symbol of her bright future.

Holly's parents, deeply saddened by their loss, were

likely successful and well-educated, raising five children with love and care. The Mini Coupe, given as a gift for her high school journey, only adds to the profound sense of loss over the future she will never experience.

Holly's father tearfully shared a message with her friends. His daughter had left a note asking her mother not to be too surprised and to carry on as if nothing had happened. But her father wanted to remind everyone that no family can ever live as if nothing happened after such a loss. Instead, they will carry the pain for the rest of their lives, and he urged Holly's friends not to make choices that would bring such overwhelming grief to their own families.

Holly's parents had noticed a troubling change in her behavior about eight months earlier. The notebook she used for solving math problems and taking notes had several blank pages, a detail that puzzled them. They later discovered that she had been meeting with the school counselor. The parents gently suggested that schools should immediately inform families of such important matters, stressing that early intervention could make a difference.

It's heartbreaking—what makes these young lives with so much potential end before they even begin to bloom? In Silicon Valley, where many parents have achieved the highest levels of education, it can be difficult for children to match their parents' success. There's a belief that if a student falls behind academically, even slightly, they may feel trapped in a cycle of perceived failure, which can tragically lead to extreme decisions.

Yet, the uncertainty of the future, even if it involves pain, is precisely what makes life worth living.

For young people struggling in silence, trapped in their own tragic narratives, I wish to offer them the wisdom from a Simon and Garfunkel song:
"A Bridge Over Troubled Water"—Friends, I will be that bridge for you. Please, step on me and cross over.

Reflections on the Year's End

2017-11-25 (Sat)

It's a time when I should be immersed in happiness, enjoying the carols that start playing in full after Thanksgiving, but my heart is unsettled. News of the earthquake in Pohang, a city in my home country, has dampened my mood. I should be humming along, thinking, *"This is enough. I just hope to stay healthy for the rest of the year,"* but a part of me feels heavy.

As the festive season approaches, filled with gratitude and holiday cheer, everyone around me seems excited, walking faster and more impatiently. I drove to Costco to pick up snacks for everyone—bananas, Dungeness crabs, and a bottle of vodka. This "close friend" of mine, with 41% alcohol, sends a chill through me, like a 5.4 magnitude earthquake in my stomach, when I take a sip once or twice a week. Most importantly, I went to fill up on gas, which is definitely cheaper than at regular stations.

Even when I'm anxiously awaiting news on a pending contract, instead of bothering clients with phone calls, I prefer to wander around Costco, lost in thought and calming my mind. The only downside is that my phone's charge only lasts about five hours. But with a Bluetooth headset that has great sound quality and sleek design, making calls while shopping is still a pleasant change of pace for me.

When I pulled into the parking lot, it was packed with holiday shoppers. After circling a few times in search of a spot, I decided to wait for a car that was nearly loaded up and ready to leave. I turned on my lights and patiently waited. But what happened next? A car, full of kids and clearly arriving after me, swooped in closer and cut in front of me, despite knowing I was already waiting.

Aarrgghhhh... I honked my horn reflexively. No matter how tough the situation, I usually keep my cool. But it's hard to tolerate behavior like that. Maybe if people learn that acting rudely gets them called out, they'll think twice before stepping outside the bounds of civility.

After finishing my shopping, I remembered a message from my dearest, most brilliant friend, who is more like a younger brother, Dr. Quan—a Chinese a primary care doctor at Kaiser Hospital. I decided to drive over to the hospital in downtown Mountain View, where Google's headquarters is located.

As the song says, *"Who can stop the passage of time?"* Even I, with a well-trained body and physical strength from years of swimming during the week and long-distance running on weekends, find myself powerless against the relentless process of aging.

I've always been confident in my health, even able to read relatively small print without a magnifying glass. But at some point, high blood pressure crept up on me, and now I feel its effects. It's been two months since I was first prescribed blood pressure medication, a milestone in my life. I asked Dr. Quan if I should continue taking it, and he responded through the hospital's secure email system.

His advice was to continue the medication for another month and a half, until the end of the year, even if I managed to lose just five more pounds. Then, we would reassess my blood pressure at the start of the new year.

Earlier this year, when I moved to an office without a free soda service, I stopped drinking the four cans of refreshing Coke I used to have daily. As a result, I lost 10 pounds in 10 months. It turns out that some "friendly" free services aren't so friendly to your body.

To lose another five pounds, I know I need to break my final bad habit: my late-night spicy ramen addiction. The sodium in the ramen broth, which exceeds the daily recommended amount, causes excess water to be absorbed into the bloodstream. This increases blood volume, putting strain on the heart and kidneys, and is a major contributor to high blood pressure. Cutting back is essential.

With only about a month left in the eventful year of 2017, I'd like to send my deepest condolences and warmest thoughts to the people of Pohang, who have endured the worst earthquake damage and are now grappling with fear and uncertainty.

Chapter 3

Fight On, Together!

"Fight on!"

2017-12-30 (Sat)

Ka~talk! The phone buzzed with the Sound of a message alert. The office, nearly deserted as most tenants are away on long year-end vacations, is suddenly filled with the sound of a message notification, startling me from a light doze. I glance at my phone screen—it's a message from my younger son, who lives in LA. My son, who works as an accountant and internal auditor at a commercial real estate investment company in Hollywood, has sent me a single-character reply: "Yes."

Filial piety, friendship, and love are principles that should never have to be asked for, but as the season of reflection and longing arrives, I couldn't resist checking in with my son—who's been working hard and hasn't been able to come home—just to ask if he loves his father. After 12 long hours, this was his response.

There's much I can learn from my son's laid-back nature. Whether it's an email, message, or comment, I feel the need to respond immediately, appreciating the sincerity of the sender. Sometimes, though, I wonder if I'm being too hasty, too shallow in my eagerness.

In truth, we each have a personal "thermometer" for measuring the temperature of our relationships with others—how deeply we engage, how quickly we reply, and whether we show respect in every message we send. We assess these relationships almost instinctively, faster than the speed of light.

My son probably got home late after a Friday night year-end party with friends, slept in, and then sent me his reply. I smile, remembering myself at his age. My precious, easygoing son... Though our exchange was brief, just a single word, it was enough to convey a deep understanding of each other's lives. What a beautiful connection it is to meet as a parent and child in this world.

After completing the last underwater survival class of the year at the YMCA, the members gathered in the lobby, chatting over hot coffee about their company year-end parties and upcoming ski trips to Lake Tahoe.

Among the eight members, three have family members who work at Apple. Apple, despite recently losing its top spot to Google, remains the most valuable company in Silicon Valley, with a market capitalization of $900 billion. Two of the women's husbands, both lawyers, hold PhDs in computer science and work as senior engineers at Apple. Meanwhile, Adrian, a Chinese man in his late 30s, is a global parts sourcing manager for the tech giant.

Apple, raking in huge profits, hosted lavish year-end parties for each division at the Ritz-Carlton, a luxury hotel perched on a cliff along the Pacific coast at Half Moon Bay. Even family members were invited to enjoy a feast of gourmet food, with a $10,000 cash prize up for grabs. The scene must have been buzzing with excitement.

But when it was Richard's turn to speak—Richard, the leader of our swim team and a high-ranking executive at a venture company offering internet subscription services for all kinds of Magazines like Netflix does for movies—his face grew dark, and my heart sank for him. He shared that his company's performance had been poor, and as a result, there was no year-end bonus or party, leaving a heavy silence in the office. He felt for his demoralized employees, and he was embarrassed that he had to console them in such circumstances.

He admitted that he sometimes wakes up at dawn, feeling a dark shadow looming over his future despite his high salary. With a sigh, he added that he couldn't even imagine taking a year-end trip to Taiwan, where his wife's family lives. Though he owns a beautiful $3 million home in Palo Alto, he constantly worries about the mortgage and property taxes.

Then he turned to me, expressing envy that I don't have subordinates to worry about giving bonuses to or superiors watching my every move when performance slips. The words, *Richard, though I am an owner, but you don't know the hardships of a one-man business—no guarantees, irregular income, and full responsibility for everything"* hurt me a lot, but I chose to keep quiet.

Tomorrow, the year 2017—marked by N. Korea's nuclear tests and missile threats—will fade into the back alleys of history. Let's set aside both regrets and joys, open our hearts, and proudly welcome the Year of the Dog, 2018. I'm reminded of the motto of my son's alma mater, USC: *Fight on!*

Richard, my swimming buddy of 15 years, no matter what challenges come your way, never give up. Fight until the very end! *Fight on!*

A year Begins with Reconciliation

2018-02-03 (Sat)

I have a good feeling about the coming year, as one wonderful event after another has unfolded since the start of the year. Just a few days ago, I was invited to a delightful dinner at a Chinese restaurant in downtown Berkeley. I enjoyed what was said to be the best Peking duck in Northern California, all while riding in a luxury Porsche SUV driven by an essayist and painter from the San Francisco Writers' Association.

Everyone feels deeply grateful when they encounter someone who truly values them. It's not often that we're invited to such special occasions in life. Furthermore, it takes a certain grace to be the one to extend an invitation first and arrange such a thoughtful gathering.

If you have the freedom to reflect on life and a philosophy that treasures meaningful encounters, you'll find yourself drawn to particular people—and even have the privilege of inviting them over and treating them well. I'm grateful that I am someone others want to meet.

Sixteen years ago, when I immigrated to Silicon Valley for work and took on the role of branch manager at a Korean bank, I heard rumors about a famous female novelist living nearby. A petite but sharp-eyed older woman, a regular customer, would stop by my desk after completing her business at the bank and greet me warmly. It wasn't long before I learned that she was indeed a novelist.

The staff informed me that Ms. Shin Yeasun had published an autobiographical novel with the intriguing title, *Etrange, Where is Your Homeland?* 35 years ago. At the time of its release, I was just an elementary school boy, too young to understand its content, but the title and her name appeared so frequently in the media that they became imprinted in my young mind.

While I was adjusting to my new job in an unfamiliar America, I didn't have much time to read novels. Still, I went to the only Korean bookstore in San Jose, conveniently located next to my branch, to look for her books—but I couldn't find any. Later, I heard that she was serializing a novel in the *Northern California Korean Daily*.

It wasn't easy to keep up with the serialized novel in the newspaper. I was busy trying to improve the branch's sales performance, leaving little time to sit down and read the paper thoroughly. If I missed a few episodes, I would lose the connection to the larger story and only remember the title, unable to appreciate the emotional depth of the novel entirely.

This remarkable woman, an intellectual who came to Boston to study in the early 1960s when her homeland was struggling, made her literary debut in Korea with a novel that stirred up attention, portraying the joys and sorrows of immigrant life. Her work had a significant impact. Since then, she has lived a fierce life as a writer, widely interacting with renowned authors, including the late Lee Byung-joo, a great Korean novelist, as well as Nobel Prize winners from both the East and the West. Now, she is approaching her eighties.

The novelist lady still passionately leads the San Francisco Writers' Association and holds a literary camp every summer, guiding younger writers with utmost sincerity. She is a very precious person who has steadily kept the flame of immigrant literature alive and has shed a fragrant light on literature and art in the Korean community here.

How heartwarming it must have been for such an honorable person to take a look at my weekend essay and invite me to a New Year's dinner with executives from the Northern California Korea Times America.

Looking back, it has been a long time since I had a good time enjoying a glass of fine wine and a proper meal in a classy restaurant and having a high-level conversation about literature and art. At the same time, I wasted my time getting caught up in unproductive work and feeling frustrated.

Was this all I had for the New Year? No. A few days later, I received another unexpected invitation. My eldest son, Sunghyun, who had heard through the wind that he was graduating from UC Berkeley and working at Samsung Electronics, invited me to dinner at a fancy steakhouse in Palo Alto.

It has been five years since we met again. We opened our hearts and talked and had a moment of truth where we reconciled with each other. What a beautiful and auspicious New Year's Day. I hope that all of you readers will have a wonderful time meeting and reconciling this year.

Reuniting with my Son

2018-03-10 (Sat)

There was a dimly lit restaurant building, and my heart grew heavy as I approached the meeting place. It was 8 p.m., and my son, who had been working hard at a large company, had made a late reservation and invited his father.

As I entered the restaurant, unsure of how things had changed over the years, I spotted my eldest son loitering near the entrance. Awkwardly, I shook his hand and asked how he was doing. He looked anxious.

He confessed that he had been waiting nervously for his father, whom he hadn't seen in five years. The awkwardness had become so unbearable that he was considering leaving just as we crossed paths. It was clear that time had distanced us. Despite his good height—about 183 cm—he looked thin and worn out. It must have been due to a lack of exercise, smoking, a poor appetite, and neglecting his diet while living alone.

Still, even if my son had issues with me, he shouldn't have become so cold-hearted as to cut off all contact, never reaching out—not even until my death. A nagging fear crept into my mind, reminding me of Steve Jobs's biological father, who never saw his son again.

Was that where I was headed?

No, I thought. What did I do wrong? Even as I grumbled internally, I resolved to apologize first, no matter what. What good would it do to argue over who was right or wrong between a parent and a child?

My son, now in his thirties, told me he was dating a third-generation Korean-Japanese woman. She graduated from a prestigious university and worked as a store manager for a global clothing company in Nagoya, Japan. While I was happy for him, I couldn't help but worry. Even in this Internet age, maintaining a relationship across such a distance wouldn't be easy.

Nagoya holds a special connection to our family. In 1933, during the Sino-Japanese War, my son's grandfather, then just 12 years old, left the impoverished Korean Peninsula with his father—my son's great-grandfather—who was in his mid-30s. Together, we crossed the Genkai Sea in Korea straight in search of a better life.

After settling in Osaka, my father worked in a factory and studied tirelessly day and night. His hard work paid off when, at 19, he passed the Japanese national examination to become an elementary school teacher in Japan. His first teaching post was in Nagoya.

So, when my son went to Nagoya to meet a Korean girl in the city where his grandfather once lived and worked, it felt like a full circle. Somewhere in heaven, my grandfather must have been watching, his heart filled with happiness, knowing that his legacy still lingered in that distant place.

My son finally confessed why he had been avoiding me for so long. It was because of the beatings he endured during middle school in Korea and the heartbreak of having to leave behind his life in Bundang after his second year that he felt popular among his friends to come to the United States. That transition hurt him deeply.

As I reflect on those times, I remember hitting him. He was going through puberty, and whenever his mother said something he didn't like, he would lash out so violently that peace seemed impossible in our home.

I wish I had handled it differently. When I started glaring at him to signal my disapproval of his behavior, I expected him to stop making noise. However, he didn't, and despite my warning, he continued—ultimately leading me to slap him in an attempt to make him stop.

People of my generation couldn't even imagine talking back to their parents. Growing up in poverty, with my tuition often overdue, I endured the humiliation of being singled out during class assemblies.

One day, frustrated with my father for always paying my sister's tuition first and refusing my request to pay mine first just once, I did something unthinkable—I ran away from home right in front of my parents.

The cold night air stung as I wandered through Donam-dong, passing by the air-raid shelters where many had died during the Korean War. Hungry and alone, I couldn't even last an hour before the desperate thoughts of dinner forced me back home. That was the extent of my rebellion, and it was hard for me to show leniency toward my son's defiance when he would shout, "If you love America so much, Dad, go by yourself!"

I sincerely apologized to my son, admitting that I had been an inexperienced, young father. He accepted my apology with grace, and we had a dramatic reconciliation, finally restoring our father-son relationship.

Looking back, I regret many things. When my son, then in his third year of middle school, asked me to buy him a cell phone during our early days of immigration, I hesitated too long. I delayed again when he asked for an electronic English dictionary, leaving him anxious.

Though I regret it now, life moves forward like an arrow, and here I am in my late 50s, realizing that the golden opportunities to make my children happy will never return. If given another chance, I would do everything possible to bring joy to my children.

But now, my son, I must pass on the love I couldn't give you to my future grandchild. So, you've no choice—you must get married soon!

The Shanghai Twist

2018-04-14 (Sat)

Q owns three houses in the East Bay but has been living in Palo Alto, known for its top-rated school district, to ensure the best education for her two mixed-race white daughters. As her daughters moved into middle and high school, the house became too small, so she decided to upgrade to a larger home for the same price. She rented the back house of my longtime swimming buddy at Y—an elderly Taiwanese woman—and signed a three-year lease, planning to move in early July.

Q is a proud, independent woman who graduated from Shanghai Jiaotong University and now works as a team leader at an AI startup, earning a high salary. Curious about her alma mater, I asked a friend who graduated from Beijing Medical University, given its name, if it specialized in railway transportation. She explained that it no longer has anything to do with transportation and is now considered one of the top 180 universities worldwide. He also mentioned that former Chinese President Jiang Zemin is a notable alumnus.

As I think of Shanghai, I time-traveled back to the night streets of the city I visited 24 years ago, in 1994, when I attended a banking conference there.

At that time, China was still in its early stages of development, far from being part of the G-20. From the historic European-style The Bund Waidan Street, a foreign-leased area along the Huangpu River, you could see Pudong, which the Chinese proudly touted as a new development. However, it was a wasteland, except for one tall building with a spire—the Dongfengmingzhu (Oriental Pearl TV Tower).

In the alley markets, vendors made *hotteoks on carts, and hand-stitched underwear was* hung on clotheslines in the residential areas. These sights stirred a sense of nostalgia in me, yet I also felt so negatively proud that China still had a long way to go in its development.

After finishing our business for the day, we explored the Shanghai's Korean Provisional Government Building during Japanese colonial ruling and the bustling streets of Nanjingdong Road. Still, we returned to the hotel early, feeling somewhat unsatisfied. That's when two mysterious women approached us, speaking in Japanese, and offered to take us to a lovely lounge nearby. We made the biggest mistake of our lives by accepting their offer and getting into a taxi.

We thought, *How much could they possibly overcharge us?* Our curiosity and willingness to experience Chinese nightlife blinded us. As expected, they led us to a lounge in a deserted area, and when we grew anxious and wanted to leave, they handed us a bill—$300 for four beers.

We shook our heads, saying, "Isn't that too much?" In response, they made a phone call. Moments later, gangsters arrived, each carrying brick-sized cell phones—rare and intimidating at the time. They quickly surrounded us, and we realized things were taking a turn for the worse.

We tried to offer what we had, hoping to resolve the situation, but they kept increasing. In the end, we were robbed of $1,100, including cash and traveler's checks we had hidden in our socks.

$1,100 for four beers... Unbelievable. But despite the shock, I'm grateful to be alive and able to write this recollection from the safety of Silicon Valley. A visibly shaken group member trembled like an aspen leaf and began to stutter when he caught sight of a flashing knife tucked inside the inner pocket of one of the villain's jackets.

Afterward, they shoved us into a taxi and drove us down a dark, unfamiliar road. When they eventually stopped at the end of a pitch-black alley, they told us to get out. Instinctively, we knew getting out meant we wouldn't survive. A tense struggle ensued, with them trying to open the doors from the outside and us pulling desperately from the inside. After about five minutes of this terrifying tug-of-war, we finally let go of the handle and attempted to escape.

As I watched them roll onto the road, I sprinted at full speed through the deserted back alleys of Shanghai. With legs conditioned from 20 years of running 10 km every weekend, I ran with all my might, not daring to look back for about 500 meters. But the sound of footsteps behind me never seemed to fade. *I thought, no... I'll have to fight to the death.* Clenching my fist, I turned around, ready to strike—only to find it was my friend who had escaped with me.

Relieved, we continued down the dark road and waved frantically for another taxi. Eventually, we returned to the hotel, exhausted, just after 2 AM.

A week after safely returning to Korea, I nearly fainted when I read the morning paper: *'Korean on a business trip at Shanghai Hongqiao Hotel attacked and killed by robbers.'* My body shook with fear.

That harrowing experience taught me a once-in-a-lifetime lesson: never trust strangers with your safety in unfamiliar places. Despite the cheerful tune of *'Shanghai, Shanghai, dancing the twist~,'* some corners of the world are far less romantic than they seem.

My Apology to Victor

2018-05-19 (Sat)

Victor Chen, a Chinese-American who previously worked as a Google engineer, now holds a senior engineer position at Coupang's Silicon Valley research center, a Korean-owned e-commerce company. Mr. Chen, in his early 40s, called out to me from the jacuzzi as I passed by, likely recalling our conversation from the day before.

The day prior, I had been in a heated discussion with Bharat, an Indian psychiatrist in his mid-50s, while in the sauna. We were debating the movements of the North Korean regime ahead of the North Korea-U.S. summit when Victor walked in and joined the conversation.

We speculated about the urgent and undisclosed reasons why Chairman Kim Jong-un had returned to China to meet with President Xi Jinping just 40 days after their previous meeting. Our discussion began with a light guess: perhaps Kim, likely in his early 30s and with little diplomatic experience, sought advice and encouragement from President Xi on handling the stress of meeting with President Trump—a leader of a superpower and an unpredictable figure.

Our conversation had ventured into speculation that North Korea might have secretly discussed plans to rearm its nuclear weapons in case of an emergency. The idea was that they could hide their arsenal to evade Western nuclear inspections while using a historic meeting with President Trump to eliminate economic sanctions and secure massive financial aid.

Victor had walked in just as Bharat, the elite psychiatrist, jokingly suggested that China might have been acting as a proxy, storing North Korea's nuclear weapons. In this scenario, if North Korea found itself cornered, it could launch the weapons from China at the push of a button.

Given the tense history between China and India, including their recent border disputes, we were all aware that such a conversation could carry subtle undercurrents of confrontation between the two nations. Realizing the potential awkwardness, we continued our discussion cautiously. After a while, I excused myself and left.

Victor, who had been listening silently, seemed to scold Bharat afterward. He pointed out that it would be better to avoid conversations where one's country of origin is cast in a negative light. His displeasure was clear as he asked Bharat how he would feel if someone were to publicly bring up the troubling reports of serial rapes and murders in India.

I, who had been listening, chimed in, "That makes perfect sense. Yesterday, I made a mistake by not interrupting the conversation when you entered. I was awkward and didn't want to disrupt it, but I hope you can understand and forgive me."

Victor, being a reasonable and thoughtful engineer, took my hand and helped ease the tension that had been building.

As we go through life, awkward situations often arise, whether we intend them or not. This morning, I learned a simple but valuable lesson: the key to handling those embarrassing moments wisely and gracefully is not to panic and ask, *"What should I do?"* but to offer a sincere apology.

With the Korean Peninsula capturing the world's attention, my presence at the gym seems to grow daily. Even while showering, my Chinese friend Ray would call out through the curtain, "June 12th, Singapore!"—referring to the upcoming summit between North Korea and the United States.

It seems that North Korea and the U.S. have already reached agreements on most major issues. Now, all that remains is to announce a historic agreement, marking the beginning of a nuclear-free Korean Peninsula—perhaps over a Singapore Sling and a plate of chili crab.

While North Korea might hide its nuclear arsenal for the future, the issue of accepting comprehensive and complete inspections by international atomic inspectors is another matter entirely. In exchange for North Korea's complete, verifiable, and irreversible denuclearization (CVID), large-scale economic support and investments from South Korea, the U.S., and Japan will flow in. The resulting infrastructure development will inevitably lead to the opening of North Korean society, fundamentally shifting the security landscape of the Korean Peninsula. This is a development of global interest.

The world is eagerly focusing on Singapore as it anticipates next month's historic meeting between the leaders of North Korea and the United States. The hopes are high for the declaration of the Korean War's end, the Korean Peninsula's denuclearization, and the opening of a new era of inter-Korean dialogue.

Could a miracle like the reunification of Korea—a long-cherished dream of the Korean people—happen suddenly, just as it did in Germany?

Unchi Focus Lens

2018-06-23 (Sat)

"What is this? You guys decide the bombing targets, and we just watch?"

This exchange occurred on a summer day 34 years ago, less than ten days before the UFL (Ulchi Focus Lens) joint ROK-US military exercise, inside a bunker at the nuclear defense position of the Osan U.S. army airfield. Captain C, the strike target intelligence team leader of the 6th Tactical Intelligence Group—responsible for intelligence operations at Gunsan Airfield and the Osan 51st Tactical Squadron, which operated the latest F-16 fighter jets of the U.S. 7th Air Force—briefly wore a perplexed expression.

The situation was tense. Just a year prior, following the Aung San incident, relations between North and South Korea were on the brink of collapse. In October of the previous year, North Korean operatives had attempted to assassinate then-President Chun Doo-hwan during his visit to Burma. Though the attempt failed, it claimed the lives of 17 South Korean officials, including the deputy prime minister, foreign minister, and several Blue House secretaries. When the Ulchi exercise commenced, although it was just a training exercise, the entire nation entered a state of quasi-war.

As a college freshman, if my professor used original texts like *Microeconomics Theory* or *History of Science* as textbooks, I would eagerly buy them, look up unfamiliar words in an English-English dictionary, and read them diligently, though somewhat naively. After finishing each book, I would hold a small celebration—called 'Chaek-Gory'. I also took pride in my comparative advantage in English, having listened religiously to the US Forces Korea Radio (AFKN) to perfect my native-speaker pronunciation.

Even after being commissioned as an officer in the R.O.K Air Force, I continued my passion for reading. I bought popular bestsellers like Sidney Sheldon's *Master of the Game*, introduced in the U.S. military newspaper *Stars and Stripes*. On payday, I would exchange dollars at a sneaker shop outside the main gate of Osan Air Base. I would give the money to my friend, a U.S. military intelligence officer from Colorado, and ask him to purchase books from the base store for me. I studied English diligently, yet despite my efforts, it was still difficult to express myself clearly to my U.S. military counterparts in fluent, native-level English.

Listening to our interactions, Captain C must have also felt frustrated. At the time, the difference between the U.S. Air Force and the Korean Air Force—in terms of equipment and tactical operations—was like the gap between a kindergarten student and a graduate student. That disparity likely hasn't changed much, even today.

Lieutenant Kim, I, boldly argued that since this was a joint training exercise, both sides should be equally involved in creating the training plan from A to Z. I suggested that even if the schedule had to be delayed because the Korean Air Force, with its outdated systems and knowledge, couldn't keep up, they should be taught along the way. Captain C seemed perplexed by Lieutenant Kim's reasonable argument but listened patiently and tried to make me understand.

The primary purpose of stationing U.S. troops wasn't to educate or modernize the underdeveloped Korean military but rather to protect the strategic interests of both South Korea and the U.S. with maximum efficiency.

The issue of modernizing the Korean military isn't something that can be solved easily by presidents, past or present, simply shouting at the military, *"What have the generals been doing, spending so much of the defense budget without developing the capability to recover even a single bit of operational control from USFK?"*

Even countries like Germany and the UK, which host U.S. military bases, conduct annual NATO joint military exercises under U.S. leadership. This doesn't imply they lack ownership or military capability.

It was exciting and tense to meet the U.S. naval officers—men and women—who had just disembarked from aircraft carriers or submarines that docked at Busan Port for the training exercise. Alongside them were fighter pilots, gunners, and pilots of the B-52 strategic bombers deployed from Guam and Okinawa, with whom we conducted joint military operations. Even though it was just training, it gave us valuable insights into how to strengthen our national defense capabilities.

During shift changes every 12 hours, we always briefed the incoming team on any unusual movements by the North Korean military. Officers from the Army, Navy, and Air Force reported on the current status of North Korea's land, sea, and air forces. In contrast, the Korean

Air Force officers handled the sequential interpretation.

After the North Korea-U.S. summit in Singapore, the U.S. abruptly canceled the joint South Korea-U.S. military exercise Ulchi Freedom Guardian (UFG), scheduled for July to create a friendlier atmosphere. This marked the first cancellation in 28 years, the last being in 1990 due to the Iraq War.

It's said that President Trump first proposed this to North Korea, but it's still unclear which side made the bigger concession to make the summit happen. Regardless, I sincerely hope that this time, North Korea will demonstrate its sincerity by implementing trustworthy follow-up measures and moving toward peace and prosperity, all under the security of the U.S. regime.

"Ah, San Diego!"

2018-08-04 (Sat)

"Piña Colada!" I eagerly call out to the handsome bartender, sitting on the outdoor terrace of a beach bar with the midsummer sun warming my back. The sweet, alcoholic aroma spreads through my body as I peer through my sunglasses at bikini-clad vacationers strolling along the expansive, white, sandy Coronado Beach, which seems to stretch for at least 4 km from north to south.

This is the historic Hotel Coronado del Sol, built 130 years ago in 1888 when Korea's Joseon Dynasty struggled in the darkness of political upheaval from the Im-o Incident and the Gapsin Coup. The hotel is a San Diego icon, so much so that Queen Elizabeth of England visited on her royal yacht in 1976 to host a luncheon celebrating the 200th anniversary of American Independence. I imagine the queen, as she dined in this former colony, reflecting on the faded glory of the British Empire.

It's a far cry from the Guinness stout I used to enjoy while listening to live acoustic guitar at an Irish pub in the basement of the Chosun Hotel, surrounded by the skyscrapers of downtown Seoul, some 20 years ago—before I immigrated. As for this cocktail? I'm not a cocktail enthusiast, but I learned about it by asking the American couple sitting next to me what they were drinking. Their drinks looked so appealing that I wrote down the names one by one.

Piña Colada. Squeeze lime into creamy coconut juice, pour in two types of rum—dark and light—shake vigorously, drop in a plum-colored grape with a cross cut in its skin, and garnish with a thin slice of pineapple. Two sips of pina colada were enough to make me realize that even a tall guy like me isn't immune to its effects.

This is my second time visiting San Diego. Three years ago, I only stayed for one night with my younger son, who works in LA. We visited Sea World and had a meal at a famous barbecue restaurant, but I didn't get the chance to explore the city properly.

This 9-night, 10-day stay, a rare mix of work and vacation, has given me the chance to truly appreciate San Diego's beauty and the friendliness of its people. Knowing I hadn't had a proper vacation since my trip to Korea two and a half years ago, it feels as if God blessed me with this unexpected and wonderful visit.

However, my trusty laptop, after six years of service, has begun to show clear signs of aging. I had to bring it to San Diego and even attach an external keyboard like a lifeline just to use it. Soon, though, it began signaling that its days were numbered—logging in became a challenge, as the password field endlessly filled with the number 4 as if the device had developed a mind of its own.

We bravely stopped by Costco and bought a new laptop with the latest specs. Its performance is so impressive that it feels like driving a Lamborghini—the best sports car that can accelerate from 0 to 100 miles per hour in just three seconds. My old, thick Toshiba laptop, you worked hard for six years!

Next on my list was La Jolla Cove, a popular tourist destination in San Diego known for its breathtaking sunsets. As I arrived, a small exclamation escaped my lips. In this picturesque bay, with the scent of deep green seaweed, sea lions swam gracefully among scuba divers and snorkelers against a fiery sunset. Then, as if nothing had happened, they climbed onto the shore's rocks to rest.

La Jolla's stunning scenery rivals that of Monterey in Central California, and it feels like a natural marine safari where sea lions and people coexist. I once thought the best sight was watching sea lions on San Francisco's Pier 39, roaring as they climbed onto the artificial decks. But La Jolla Beach, where you can observe sea lions climbing from the rocks just a meter away, is truly magnificent.

San Diego, a border city 500 miles south of San Francisco, shares its southern boundary with Mexico. To put it in perspective for the Korean Peninsula, it's like the distance from Sinuiju to Busan and then to Tsushima Island. The flight took just 1 hour and 20 minutes. I often saw fit and healthy sailors running around the San Diego Naval Base, home to the U.S. Pacific Fleet Command, which commands the world's largest ocean.

I've fallen in love with this beautiful city, where public safety feels secure. I'll be back soon. I love you, San Diego!

As Autumn Arrives

2018-09-08 (Sat)

'The yellow daffodils are in bloom, swaying in the wind like waves.'
Let's softly sing along to *'Daffodils'* by Hong Min, a Korean folk singer generation ago, with a rich, deep voice that stirred the emotions of our youth a generation ago. It's early morning on Labor Day when the world seems to be fast asleep.

Walking along the cloudy San Francisco Bay Trail, I descend to the quiet beach path. Before me, a spectacular sight unfolds—hundreds of water birds, including egrets, pelicans, mallards, and geese, peacefully swimming and enjoying their breakfast. I marvel at the abundance of fish and aquatic life that sustains all these birds, once again amazed by the harmony of the marine ecosystem's food chain.

It's a typical public holiday, with fitness centers, Costco, and most other businesses closed, leaving the world eerily deserted. It's as if there's a sense of urgency, a feeling that free time will be hard to come by unless you venture somewhere.

Though the cost of living is high, San Francisco has a unique charm. The city captivates us from the winding hills of Lombard Street to the iconic cable cars that seem to carry us not just over the mountains but up to the heavens. Cruise ships glide around the Golden Gate Bridge, shrouded in clouds, before returning to the docks. San Francisco's history is just as fascinating—from the infamous mafia boss Al Capone, imprisoned on Alcatraz until 1938, to the daring 1962 escape, when three prisoners made dolls out of bread, broke through walls, and vanished without a trace for over 50 years.

San Francisco is a city full of stories, where beauty and mystery coexist.

With fall fast approaching, it's becoming rare to see anyone in sleeveless clothes except those jogging along the Shoreline. After waiting about five minutes in the pricey Fisherman's Wharf area, I was lucky enough to find someone leaving a free parking spot and quickly parked my car. I went to Ghirardelli Square, famous for its chocolate, bought some, and let myself get swept up in the crowd of tourists.

Needing a break, I stopped at a quiet Starbucks, ordered an Americano—rich with coffee aroma—and used the opportunity to recharge both my dead smartphone and my soul, which hadn't had coffee all day. I rummaged through my backpack, pulled out *Hillbilly Elegy,* a book I recently purchased, and began reading. I couldn't keep carrying it around without actually diving in.

The book is an autobiographical account of a 34-year-old Yale Law School graduate, now building a successful career as a venture capitalist in Silicon Valley. I bought it after seeing it featured in the *Korea Times America.* I was immediately drawn in by the humble preface, where the author expresses embarrassment about publishing an autobiography at such a young age, noting that he is neither a famous politician nor a mainstream Anglo-Saxon white Protestant (WASP).

In the 18th century, Celtic immigrants from Scotland and Ireland settled in the New World, making their homes in the mountains of Kentucky, Ohio, and the Appalachian region. These mountain people, often referred to as hillbillies, rednecks, or white trash, are described as living even more pessimistic lives than Hispanic immigrants or African Americans, trapped by drugs and inherited poverty.

As I turn the pages, I'm eager to dive into the author's honest account of how he escaped the grip of poverty, graduated from Yale Law School, and rose to success as a venture capitalist in Silicon Valley. I'm quite excited about it.

I find myself so addicted to social media platforms like Facebook that I post, read, or comment whenever I have a free moment. It's been so long since I last took the time to quietly sit down and turn a book's pages.

With Labor Day behind us and summer officially over, we've entered the autumn harvest season. Just as the author of this book soared beyond the shackles of hillbilly poverty through relentless effort, I, too, want to step away from the distractions of social media and enrich my soul through reading and contemplation this autumn.

Chapter 4

The Dew on the Rose

Jerry's Secret Diary

2018-10-13 (Sat)

The other day, I came across some pleasant medical news. It suggested that the symptom of forgetting things isn't an early sign of dementia but rather a result of the brain's active intellectual activity. I smiled faintly when I saw a humorous comment: *"See, I told you so!"*

Recently, the most talked-about news has been the dramatic series of events surrounding the confirmation hearings and nomination of Supreme Court Justice Brett Kavanaugh. Professor Ford, a psychology professor at a university here in Silicon Valley, stirred controversy when she brought up a sexual assault incident from 30 years ago, informing a Democratic senator shortly after Kavanaugh's nomination. Her actions were politically interpreted, but if she had submitted a diary or memoir containing her feelings from that time, the situation might have unfolded differently.

If Trump's Supreme Court nominees had not been confirmed ahead of the midterm elections in November, it would have dealt a significant blow to her leadership. This is especially critical as she faces major issues, including North Korea's nuclear program and China's aggressive expansionist policies—like building an airstrip on an uninhabited island in the South China Sea—which have irked the United States.

The strap on my goggles snapped after enduring a year of chlorine exposure, forcing me to stop swimming. That morning, I lay alone in the sauna, staring at the ceiling, lost in thought. I pretended not to hear when someone entered, but a familiar voice greeted me cheerfully. I looked up—it was my friend Jerry, whose sharp eyes seemed as if they could pierce through a book. I thought, *"Those eyes speak of intellect."* Jerry, a Mississippi native in his late 60s, holds a Ph.D from Caltech and has taught geophysics at Stanford for the past 30 years. We first met about five years ago at a small YMCA near Stanford, and we've become close since then.

I returned his greeting and asked how he was doing. He mentioned he was preparing for retirement in 2-3 years and had already decided what he wanted to do afterward. Intrigued, I asked what his plans were. Jerry told me he was working on a memoir, recording his thoughts on his smartphone whenever inspiration struck. Even for such a world-renowned scholar, the habit of taking notes is essential.

Jerry, who is about 10 years senior to me, also mentioned that his son is dating a mixed-race Korean woman—her father is American Indian, and her mother is Korean. He shared a story about a Korean student who married a Korean woman in Korea and had a lonely wedding without his parents. His connection to Korea seems quite remarkable.

While I don't have many opportunities to compare myself to others, I also try to take notes diligently. Whenever I hear exciting news or something noteworthy crosses my mind, I jot it down in a computer notebook, though not as rigorously as Jerry does. Still, this habit has been a great help in many aspects of my life.

Japan, a country Koreans have held grudges against for their imperialism while it has been already 73 years since liberation, has produced another Nobel Prize winner this year, this time in Physiology or Medicine.

With 25 Nobel laureates to date, Japan is solidifying its position as a valid scientific powerhouse. This success is undoubtedly built on the Japanese people's persistence, sincerity, and dedication to their studies, their renowned passion for reading, and their thorough record-keeping habits. It's time to remove outdated, negative national sentiments and learn from this severe and disciplined approach.

Persistence wins every battle. Even without a Nobel Prize, Samsung Electronics surpassed Sony and now leads the global electronics and semiconductor industries. But if we become complacent about these achievements and let our efforts slacken, the future of our country is in jeopardy.

Rather than wasting time on political revenge or inflaming anti-Japanese rhetoric, I hope that our homeland, the Republic of Korea, focuses its national energy on creating an environment where our brightest young minds can devote themselves to basic scientific research.

We risk stagnation if we don't sense the crisis when we see talented young people from low-income families flocking to exam prep study villages to become civil servants, seeking job security over innovation. Offering only small government subsidies instead of a comprehensive, 100-year job creation plan that addresses the root causes of unemployment will lead to a bleak future for our country.

I dream of the day when I hear that my homeland across the Pacific is filled with young people who, despite challenging circumstances, remain hopeful and passionate about both their careers and their conjugal lives. After all, our older generation lived with that same spirit.

Dew on That Rose....

2018-11-17 (Sat)

Ah, what a relief. After wearing them all day, taking off my Bluetooth earpiece feels refreshing—the air seems clearer, the intense tension eases, and warmth finally returns to my heart.

At 10 p.m., the only sound is the janitors doing their work, and the surroundings are quiet. Today was so hectic that I didn't even have time for my usual walk, so this moment of peace is welcome. After scanning dozens of documents, renaming them for easy access, organizing them in an easy order for others to follow, and sending them off for electronic approval, DocuSign. I finally stretched my sore legs. At that moment, I feel a slight sense of happiness. ***Jininsa Daecheonmyeong** is a Korean/Chinese saying that means "Do your best and wait for heaven's help."*

While taking a breather, I watched a piano solo of the hymn "Dew on the Roses," which was sent to me by a friend in Seoul on YouTube. A sense of peace gently rises in my heart like a soft mist, as if the Lord is comforting me for my hard work today.

The video was sent by an elementary school friend of 40 years. Whenever I visit Seoul, especially since my parents passed away, he welcomes me with a sumptuous feast and wine at his home. The video featured his son, majoring in piano in the U.S., playing a special performance at their church during a short visit back to Korea. It was graceful and beautiful.

Earlier in the day, amidst the chaos, I received a lunch invitation just 30 minutes before the break. It was from my senior, Branch Manager L, whom I worked with as a fellow branch manager at same Korean bank in Northern California during my early years of immigration. Nearing 70, he continued his banking career for nearly 40 years, and now he works at an American bank. He's a living testament to the history of Korean banking in Northern California, showing us all what perseverance indeed looks like.

After working in LA for four years, he returned to San Francisco. Despite his busy banking career, he always finds time to be an insightful commentator on radio and TV, which never fails to inspire me.

As he was heading back from a TV recording in San Jose, I suddenly crossed his mind. The moment he invited me to lunch; I bolted out like a bullet. After all, isn't it a "Lightning," and one doesn't need an appointment for that?

For clarity, a Lightning Call or Meeting refers to a Korean way of suddenly meeting friends for eating and drinking without an appointment. I was overjoyed to experience something so meaningful—something I truly cherish.

Lately, I've come to feel just how short life is. That's why I try to respond to important people, no matter how urgent the message or how far away they are. I also think it's crucial to reach out to those who have impacted me or whom I think about often, expressing my gratitude at the right time so that life doesn't become mundane.

I immigrated in my early 40s and am now approaching my 60s. Time has passed like a dream. When I think about how quickly time will continue to pass and that I'll soon be in my late 70s, approaching 80, I can't help but get lost in thought.

This past week has been heartbreaking, with the Camp Fire—the largest wildfire in California's history—claiming nearly 60 lives, with hundreds more still missing in the retirement community of Paradise, 250 miles north.

Despite the tragedies around me, I stayed busy with work. But outside of work, I found one small reward: I finally finished *Hillbilly Elegy*, the autobiography of a young lawyer, after two months of weekend reading. The book, written in English, took me a while to complete, but it was worth it.

The author, one of the few successful "hillbillies," escaped extreme poverty. Despite his challenging childhood, he went on to serve in the Marine Corps, graduate from Yale Law School, and become a highly-paid lawyer at a prestigious firm, joining the elite circles of American society. When he visited his hometown, he met Brian, a young boy separated from his biological parents and living under foster care, much like the author's own past. He felt deep compassion for him.

The author, who never expected much from his book, found himself unexpectedly making a fortune when the first edition—initially projected to sell only 10,000 copies—ended up selling 2 million. With the proceeds, he was able to build a small mountain for the use of a cemetery for his ancestors in his poverty-stricken hometown in Kentucky, a place marked by broken families and deep distrust between neighbors. At that moment, I couldn't help but silently applaud.

Now that the year is nearly over, I'm wondering—what book should I pick up next? Perhaps Jane Austen's *Pride and Prejudice*?

"Hello, Amir!"

2018-12-22 (Sat)

"Doug, I've been relocated. Let's keep in touch." My first Egyptian friend, Amir, who had been quietly managing his bases in two Silicon Valley locations—Cupertino and Menlo Park—shook my hand with a hint of sadness when he showed up after a long absence.

Amir is a gentle, good-natured friend who runs a startup that uses AI to process big data. His desk was right next to mine. He graduated from NYU at 22 and has been running multiple companies for 17 years. He came with his CTO to move supplies into their car that day.

This time, they secured nearly $1 million in funding, so they decided to expand their Cupertino office, hire more staff, and consolidate operations there. While I enjoyed working alongside him once or twice a week, having more space while he was away was also nice. "Amir, you were the best neighbor. You couldn't have been quieter," I said, and he laughed with a childlike, unpretentious smile.

In a co-working space, where many share the office, not everyone is as quiet and considerate as Amir. There are also colleagues like Raj, an Indian engineer in his early 40s who frequently chats with his team. In a calm work environment, short, low-toned business conversations are acceptable, but when it comes to long phone calls or extended discussions, common courtesy is to step into a conference room, head outside, or retreat to your own car.

I waited, hoping the conversation would stop soon, but they kept talking excitedly for over 30 minutes, making it impossible to focus on my work. These days, many startup entrepreneurs are using shared office spaces. I've heard that companies like Uber, the ride-sharing giant, and Airbnb, which revolutionized accommodations, emerged from this industry.

One such company making waves is WeWork, which has recently gained attention through Facebook ads. The name itself is friendly and straightforward—*We work.* Founded in New York in 2010, the company opened its second headquarters last November by leasing three floors, from the 36th floor upward, in the ultra-modern 61-story Salesforce Tower in San Francisco's Financial District. As soon as WeWork began expanding its business in the Bay Area, 350 out of 700 available desks were sold out almost instantly.

If I lived in San Francisco, I'd probably rent a WeWork co-working space right away—imagine working with a stunning view of both the Golden Gate Bridge and the Bay Bridge from the 36th floor. SoftBank Chairman Masayoshi Son(Son Jeong-ui), now Japan's richest man, participated in a $500 million Series B investment for

WeWork's Chinese business in August. By November, he had pledged $3 billion, pushing WeWork's valuation to $45 billion.

WeWork.com, once a somewhat unfamiliar company, has quickly risen to become the second most valuable startup, thanks to Chairman Son's investment, trailing only Uber, which holds the top spot with a valuation of $72 billion. It's fascinating to wonder how far the revolutionary wave of the sharing economy will go.

Time passes so swiftly, much like the fleeting feeling of a month-long winter vacation from my youth. How can it not? With only one week left in the year, I take a moment to reflect on the year of the dog, 2018, which will soon fade into history.

Looking back, I'd give the year an above-average rating overall. There were precious encounters, and although I couldn't meet everyone in person, the kind phone calls from cherished people warmed a corner of my otherwise dry heart.

The disappointment of a project I'd worked hard on not going as planned was soon replaced with greater joy when an unexpected phone call came from a different direction. Meeting kind and genuine people always makes my heart race a little faster.

As we close the year, I want to offer comfort to the loved ones who experienced both highs and lows, and with an open heart, I look forward to the unknown possibilities 2019—the year of the pig—will bring. I welcome it with anticipation and excitement.

Red-crowned Crane

2019-01-26 (Sat)

"It didn't happen naturally. I went through countless job interviews, faced rejection, and often experienced disappointment. But through perseverance and building my career, I finally secured a stable position at Apple. Now, I'm on the other side of the table, interviewing candidates and deciding who will contribute to the organization."

This conversation occurred in the hotel's banquet hall, where a group of 63 people—50 students and their advisors—were welcomed for a week-long Silicon Valley tour. The school fully covered the travel expenses for these junior students from my alma mater. As the local alum association president, I had the honor of participating in the event. The students' eyes sparkled with curiosity as they listened to their seniors' candid and practical experiences, who had navigated various paths to reach their positions in Silicon Valley.

Life in the San Francisco Bay Area, where talent and tourists from all over the world converge, is not always filled with rosy fantasies. It requires intense self-development and survival strategies—something that resonates with anyone, not just visiting students. These invaluable stories will serve as guiding principles for the juniors, who will soon face fierce competition in the global technology arena after completing their studies. The stories of seniors excelling in various fields continued throughout the event.

"No, you rejected me..." confessed a famous dancer, an alumna who had confidently crossed the Pacific Ocean 17 years ago to audition—only to face rejection. Despite her illustrious career, which included winning first place at the Dong-A Competition and serving as the principal dancer at the National Dance Company of Korea, her journey had been filled with obstacles.

Had she not humbly accepted that failure reflected on herself and used it as an opportunity to try again, she would not have gone on to win the Isadora Duncan Award, the highest honor in the dance world. Nor would she have been nominated for the award again 13 years later.

Another alumna, an engineer, brought actual semiconductor wafers and finished chips to illustrate the concept of semiconductors to her juniors. Next alumna appeared on the podium. After graduating from the College of Liberal Arts, she came to the U.S. for further studies and now runs a consulting company specializing in the semiconductor electronics industry. Her dynamic presentations as she moves through Silicon Valley resonate with the students, leaving a lasting impression.

The alumni stories continued to unfold: senior researcher working on rare disease treatments at Stanford University School of Medicine, doctor overseeing professors at the Monterey Defense Language School, and engineers from Qualcomm—leaders in mobile phone chip technology—Broadcom, which produces critical short-range communication components, and Nvidia, known for its core chips powering the booming autonomous vehicle industry.

The two hours we had promised flew by, filled with these inspiring stories. As we bid unwanted farewells, we offered words of encouragement to our juniors as they prepared for their own journeys.

The indomitable spirit of resilience, the refusal to yield to failure, is the secret behind Korea's rise as a globally recognized advanced nation. Some young Koreans, who waste their youth in self-mockery by calling it "Hell Joseon," need to shift their mindset and strengthen their mental resolve.

Our seniors, who faced starvation even after graduating from colleges left in ruins by the Korean War, did not waste their time waiting for government subsidies or blaming others. Instead, they went to the harshest, most difficult places, shedding blood, sweat, and tears. They descended 1,000 meters underground into West German coal mines, drenched in sweat as they dug for coal. The white-clad angelic nurses washed the dead bodies of Germans, enduring the foul stench and wiping away their tears. Other seniors risked their lives by joining the Vietnam War, earning blood-stained U.S. Dollars that became the foundation for Korea's growth.

Time has flown by like a dream, and nearly 40 years have passed since I walked along Daeseong-ro, campus drive, to the school classroom by the Changgyeong-gung Palace's stone wall road. At the age of 33, I went on my first overseas trip—a dream-like journey awarded to me by my company for being one of an excellent employees—to Guam, a U.S. territory in the Western Pacific.

Despite various crises, the Korean economy has continued to grow. Now, it can afford to send engineering students—most under the age of 20, too young even to legally drink—on fully funded trips to Silicon Valley. This economic strength has also contributed to the boom in Japan, a country both close and distant, with 7 million Koreans traveling there each year.

This winter, the cold feels unusually sharp. Around this time, Korea would often report the arrival of the 'winter guest,' announcing the red-crowned cranes, a natural monument, flying from Siberia to the Hantan River to spend the season.

Looking back, has any life been completely smooth? After being shaped by countless experiences and paths, I now find myself as the president of the local alumni association. Soon, I'll be honored to welcome juniors—like those winter guests—and deliver a speech to a group of energetic visitors eager to hear the speakers' stories.

Like a movie, isn't life worth savoring precisely because we never know what wonderful surprises the future might hold?

Warm Soup and Jambalaya

2019-02-23 (Sat)

"Goodbye, Joe, he gotta go, me oh my oh
He gotta go-pole the pirogue go down the Bayou
His Yvonne the sweetest one, me oh my oh
Son of a gun, we'll have big fun on the Bayou
Jambalaya and a crawfish pie and fillet gumbo on of a gun, we'll have big fun on the Bayou ~"

A very famous song, Jambalaya

by Carpenters

As I reminisced about childhood memories of playing with fireworks on the first full moon of the lunar year, I came across photos of a bright full moon uploaded by my elementary school classmates in Seoul. The images, taken from the veranda of a redeveloped apartment in Donam-dong, where we used to live, brought back thoughts of my hometown. Then, when another friend shared this song after a long time, I couldn't help but dance excitedly.

My friends' updates soothed my loneliness as I spent the first full moon of the year far from home.

Looking back, I only played that thrilling fireworks game once. A neighborhood brother poked holes in a powdered milk can with nails, hung it on a wire, filled it with chopped tree branches, lit it with newspaper, and spun it around. The can become an air furnace, and the burning branches created a beautiful circle of fireworks in the night sky.

That night, I listened to *Jambalaya* by the 70s duo, the Carpenters, four times in a row. Later, after work, I played it again while sitting at my desk, savoring warm lobster soup. When the *Chicken Soup for the Soul* series was a bestseller, I wondered what chicken soup had to do with the soul.

But after taking a spoonful or two of warm soup, I soon understood. A comforting warmth spreads through my body when I sip the morning soup I've come to enjoy after 17 years in the U.S. I feel almost saintly, with a peaceful soul, like a child who can't wean off the comfort of their mother's milk. I finish the entire bowl in one sitting.

The soup I remember most from my childhood in Korea is porridge—rice porridge, to be exact. My mother would boil it and add a few drops of sesame oil and soy sauce whenever I had a bad cold. I experienced more delicious variations as I got older, like abalone porridge, but that simple dish remains special. It was my mother's way of comforting me—her "healing porridge" made to help me feel better when I was sick. Though it's far from the chicken or lobster soup I enjoy now, the sentiment is the same.

I used to think *Jambalaya* was something useless, but when I looked it up on Wikipedia, I learned it's a dish—a flavorful Louisiana rice bowl made with meat, seafood, and smoked sausage. *Filet gumbo*, also mentioned in the song, is a stew that resembles a kimchi stew, made with beef, clams, and the "holy trinity" of celery, green peppers, and onions. The broth is thickened with file powder, made from dried sassafras leaves, giving it a bold, rich flavor. I've heard that you can enjoy these dishes authentically if you visit New Orleans, so I've added New Orleans to my ever-growing bucket list.

With hits like *Top of the World*, *Yesterday Once More*, and *Sing*, the Carpenters sold over 100 million records, becoming legends. Yet, despite her success, Karen Carpenter led a short and tragic life. I was stunned to learn she died of anorexia at just 33, after only three years of marriage. Karen was a contralto, a rare and beautiful vocal range for a woman. It feels almost unfair—like God was angry, taking such an extraordinary singer from us so soon.

Perhaps it's as if God allowed us to hear the voice of an angel briefly, then took her back to heaven to comfort those struggling in this world.

After several days of rain, this morning is the coldest of the winter. In the distance, the ninth ridge of Mount Hamilton, San Jose's highest peak at 4,300 feet, is blanketed in silvery white snow, sparkling under the morning sun. It's a spectacular sight—a rare stroke of luck to witness snow here, especially with Lake Tahoe just a five-hour drive away for skiing.

At -1 degrees Celsius, it's only a slight drop, but it feels unusually cold. Compared to Seoul, where temperatures often dip to -10 degrees in winter, it's nothing. Yet, having grown accustomed to San Francisco's heavenly weather, I suppose I'm becoming a bit soft—or maybe I'm just joking.

With a bowl of warm soup in my hands, I feel happier than anyone else in the world. I whisper softly, "My friends from home, take care until we meet again."

"Oh My, Toledo!"

2019-03-23 (Sat)

The United States is currently abuzz with the scandal involving parents colluding with Rick Singer, the notorious college admissions fraudster from Newport Beach, Southern California, to secure spots at prestigious universities. Not only has the long-standing rumor—that large donations can pave the way to elite institutions—been confirmed, but now we must ask: who should be held responsible for the shattered dreams of students who failed to get into their desired schools due to this ugly scandal? This fraud involved a Harvard graduate test-taker sitting for the SAT and bribery.

It is truly disheartening to see the names of global celebrities from Silicon Valley, such as Joe Montana, the legendary quarterback who played for the San Francisco 49ers for 14 seasons and won four Super Bowls, and Laurene Powell Jobs, the wife of the late Steve Jobs, being mentioned in connection with this incident.

There was a fleeting moment when I considered that perhaps one's mental health should accept that the world isn't always honest or fair. But on the other hand, I applaud the judiciary's relentless investigation, which took years to bring these people to justice. America is not perfect, but there is hope in its self-correcting system that strives to move forward.

After my morning workout, I pick up the local paper in the lobby. Amid the Silicon Valley redevelopment frenzy, driven by the tech boom and housing shortages, a beloved grocery store in Mountain View—Google's city—is closing after 45 years.

A Danish-American runs the store I know well, and he received an offer he couldn't refuse. His wife, from Shanghai, also wants to visit her hometown. It's said that young employees of tech companies rarely buy groceries and cook, preferring to hang out with friends at restaurants or order delivery, which has caused many small and medium-sized grocers to operate at a loss for years.

"Oh my... Stop drinking and leave!"

This humorous outburst refers to former Peruvian President Alejandro Toledo, who was arrested a second time for public intoxication. At 72, he appears to have been drinking heavily at a bar, perhaps to ease his loneliness.

Toledo was the hardworking son of an ordinary family, and his connection with two Peace Corps members allowed him to study in the United States. He was a determined man, working part-time as a gas station attendant, graduating from San Francisco State University on a soccer scholarship, and eventually earning two master's degrees and a doctorate in education from Stanford University.

He, a man Peruvians were once very proud of, became the 63rd President of Peru at 53, preventing Japanese-

American former President Alberto Fujimori from serving a third term (1990–2000). During his presidency, Toledo delivered a commencement speech at his alma mater, Stanford, two years before Apple's Steve Jobs. This was likely the peak of his life.

Toledo, a Stanford-educated doctor of education, rolled up his sleeves and launched a national 100-year plan to dramatically improve Peru's poor educational system—something he had painfully experienced in his childhood. He received significant praise for groundbreaking initiatives, such as connecting elementary and middle schools to a national education network and doubling teachers' salaries.

However, teachers protested against the performance-based differential pay system, and despite the increase in student enrollment, the overall illiteracy rate and average academic achievement levels saw only minimal improvement. His grand vision for educational reform, unfortunately, remained largely unfulfilled.

I laughed because the place where he was arrested was so familiar to me: a quiet neighborhood pub just across the street from the Starbucks, where I always stopped for coffee and a plain bagel during my Sunday morning 20 km runs.

If you get drunk in a pub and the staff asks you to leave, you should comply immediately. If you act foolishly, insisting, "I'm not drunk," you'll be reported to the police and arrested—whether you're a former president or not. And without exception, you'll spend the night at the police station before being released.

During his presidency, Toledo was reportedly such a heavy drinker that his private plane became known as the "party plane." In 2017, he was indicted on charges of accepting $20 million in bribes for projects awarded to Brazilian construction companies while in office, and Interpol currently wants him.

It's disheartening that, in any country, politicians who rise from adversity to success often become embroiled in abuses of power or bribery, disappointing the very people who once cheered for them. When will we ever see leaders like India's saintly Mahatma Gandhi—respected by the people throughout their lives—who pass away without scandal or disgrace?

Make America Great Again!

2019-04-27 (Sat)

"MAGA, BOGO? It's not that I miss my mom for mostly Koreans, but it's a phrase we often hear while living in America. 'BOGO' is a friendly marketing term for (Buy One Get One), meaning if you buy one, you get one free."

But what about 'MAGA'? It is President Trump's 2016 campaign slogan, 'Make America Great Again' (MAGA), a hot topic recently.

Earlier this month, a Starbucks in second downtown Palo Alto—the birthplace of Silicon Valley—made headlines related to 'MAGA.' Because Silicon Valley is under the global spotlight, events here tend to attract national attention.

California, where immigrants make up the majority, and Silicon Valley in particular, is known for being a place where people are relatively tolerant of undocumented immigrants, oppose discrimination against sexual minorities, and pride themselves on being highly educated. It's also a place where harsh language on Twitter is common, and suspicions of sexual deviance surface regularly. The dominant democrats in the region used to blame Donald Trump for draft dodgers during the Vietnam War. As a result, it's rare to see people wearing red MAGA hats in public.

The incident occurred when a 74-year-old retiree, who had also published a book on technology, was enjoying his morning coffee while wearing a red MAGA hat over a yarmulke, the traditional Orthodox Jewish head covering. Some people quietly gave him a thumbs-up, while others walked by, offering quiet praise for his boldness. He responded, "It doesn't take that much courage to wear a Trump hat!"

However, the situation escalated when he became the target of a 46-year-old white woman who loudly insulted him, shouting, "You are a crazy racist and a Nazi!" Stunned and humiliated, the man later said he wasn't sure if it was a dream, reality, or an April Fool's joke, as it happened to be April 1st. What shocked him most was the Starbucks manager and the other customers who sat still, seemingly indifferent.

It must have felt like a surreal and absurd farce, hearing her call him a Nazi when he, a Jewish man, was wearing his yarmulke. What could have ended as a small incident went viral after the woman posted a picture of the man on her Facebook page, expressing her frustration that none of the coffee shop's customers sympathized with her. In a twist of fate, she received an outpouring of unspeakable insults on her Facebook wall, and her employer, a guitar manufacturing company, fired her from her accounting job.

The victim remarked on the irony that the person who publicly insulted him ended up being the one whose life was destroyed. It made him realize just how divided American society has become. However, he showed compassion, stating that he neither expected nor wanted her to lose her job.

The female perpetrator, shocked and upset by the unexpected fallout, traveled to Seattle, 1,400 kilometers north, to meet a friend. On her way back, she was reported missing after her whereabouts were unconfirmed for about three days. After a large-scale search, she was found safe. Overwhelmed by the situation, she had turned off her phone and cut off contact with those around her, reportedly becoming mentally unstable.

I, too, passed through a challenging phase after immigrating 17 years ago, receiving permanent residency, and eventually citizenship. That's why I support President Trump, who is working to implement immigration policies based on reasonable border management, address the astronomical trade deficit with China, and confront the North Korean nuclear crisis. I agree with his slogan, "MAGA."

In the United States, a liberal democracy where freedom of expression is a basic right, witnessing an incident where someone was absurdly insulted as a "racist" or "Nazi"—without the accuser even realizing the person was Jewish—simply because their political views didn't align, made me feel that there's still much for people to learn. Am I overthinking?

Tora, Tora, Tora!!

2019-06-01 (Sat)

His expression was filled with rage. I'm talking about Stephen, a Chinese-American man I met in the kitchen at work. He's a small-scale venture investor, and for almost a year, we had only exchanged eye contact in this shared space, where many startups are based. However, about a month ago, we shook hands and became friends. Judging by his English skills, he's likely around my age, having studied abroad for graduate school and lived here for 30 years.

When I first asked him how his investment business was going on the day we became friends, he admitted it wasn't easy. He mentioned that many of his friends who received investments ended up failing, and they would say, "Stupid!" Even though venture investing generally hopes for one success in ten or twenty, he probably meant it was unfortunate that these startups didn't grow into unicorn companies with $1 billion in sales but often closed down instead.

While not all Chinese people may be like this, Stephen is incredibly easygoing and hardworking. Sometimes, when I go to the office on weekend evenings to research and read articles in preparation for the new week, I often see him there too—eyes burning with focus, wearing a tracksuit, and with messy hair. If Hamlet's question was, "To be or not to be," Stephen's question is definitely, "To invest or not to invest?"

This morning, Stephen suddenly began criticizing Trump without me even asking. He called him a "really stupid idiot" and then compared him to a sea cucumber, a sea squirt, and other sea creatures. I had to hold back my laughter as he rambled on. Inwardly, I wondered, *Why are you so angry when you can no longer stand by and watch America being used by China?*

Tora, Tora, Tora! This was the radio code used by Japanese naval pilots on December 7, 1941, to signal the success of their mission after the surprise bombing of Pearl Harbor, Hawaii.

Did Americans on the mainland feel the same urgency then as now? While there may not be bombs falling before our eyes, there's a sense that a great confrontation of the century is unfolding.

Here in Silicon Valley, the real impact of the U.S.-China trade war is already being felt. Last night, while relaxing in the jacuzzi at the pool, I spoke to Kin, a Chinese woman in her early 50s who is involved in the business of trade with China and commercial real estate investment in California. She explained that the economic war between the U.S. and China—triggered by the U.S. announcement in early May that it would raise tariffs on Chinese goods to 25%, followed by China's immediate retaliation—has led to a significant contraction in trade between the two countries. This has caused a sharp drop in import and export volumes, and vacancy rates for storage buildings in San Francisco, Oakland, and San Jose have also increased.

She pointed out that Trump's policy was wrong, arguing that if the U.S. imposes special tariffs on Chinese products, it will directly impact the prices of goods ordinary Americans buy at Walmart, making their lives more difficult.

But I hope she understands that people know how to endure shortages during a war. For example, if Walmart raises the price of shoes, instead of buying new ones, people can simply wear their old shoes longer. Meanwhile, foreign investors who run shoe factories in China will likely leave and relocate their businesses to neighboring countries like Vietnam. As a result, the damage to the U.S. will be minimal, but China will face much greater challenges.

This woman expressed her discomfort with Trump. She had previously supported his policies, including constructing a border wall, but now, with the U.S.-China trade war affecting the global economy, she says she has withdrawn her support. She claims that Trump is merely a fighter, picking battles with every country in the world.

I wanted to tell her, *"Kin, it's because Trump is taking action where previous presidents didn't."*

In times like these, South Korea should avoid doing anything that contradicts the stance of its staunch ally, the United States, which sacrificed tens of thousands of soldiers in the Korean War to protect Korea and has opened its markets, providing the economic support needed for Korea's development. However, looking at Korea's current situation from across the Pacific Ocean, I can't help but feel a sense of concern.

The world is now caught in the midst of a silent yet fierce trade war between the United States and China.

Chapter 5

Precious Moments, Precious People

To My Dear: The Sorrow Left Behind

2019-07-06 (Sat)

It's strange. The app says it's a 3-minute drive, but 10 minutes have passed, and the car still hasn't arrived. I stare at my smartphone—it's a Lyft taxi. I check the driver's information, and he answers with a Middle Eastern accent when I call. He explains that there's a problem with the system, apologizes, and suggests I find another driver.

Did a more preferred long-distance customer show up? I wondered. I began searching for another ride, but soon my phone rang again. The driver asked if I still needed a ride and if I could wait. I agreed, and he arrived in a black Ford Focus two minutes later. The wrinkles on his forehead, two or three deep lines, suggested he was in his mid-fifties.

As we drove to my destination, the frustrated driver asked if he could call the head office for help while driving. Though I was about to suggest he wait until after dropping me off, he quickly acted friendly, and I said it was fine. People who work hard should help each other—there's no need to be overly difficult. His tired expression returned as he repeatedly shouted "Technical Service!" into the phone's automated message system. Ultimately, the call didn't connect before we reached my destination.

When I casually mentioned that restarting the smartphone often fixes system issues, he replied that he had already tried that and it didn't work. Frustrated, he complained that the Motorola smartphone he bought for $300 was a "cheap piece of trash!"

Glancing at me through the rearview mirror, he asked where I was from and when I arrived. "Seventeen years ago, South Korea," I answered. "Oh, beautiful!" he responded, and I felt his genuine appreciation for Koreans, leaving me grateful.

His name was Amir, and he had immigrated from Iran 23 years ago. Back in the late 1970s, when we were young, people in South Korea constantly heard about how poor our homeland was. Readers probably grew tired of those stories, but we often looked at oil-rich countries like Saudi Arabia and Iran with pure envy.

Despite the scorching desert heat, Korean workers in those countries slept in air-conditioned accommodations during the day, waking up in the evening when the temperatures dropped to work hard throughout the night on construction projects. Korean workers earned a reputation as one-of-a-kind, leaving a lasting impression on local leaders. These countries were very wealthy, providing Korean construction companies with much work for which we were deeply thankful.

During the reign of the Shah of Iran—before he was overthrown by the Islamic Revolution led by Ayatollah Khomeini in 1979—Iran was a major source of income and construction contracts for Korea. The gratitude was mutual, so much so that when the mayor of Tehran visited Korea in 1977, a main street in the wealthy district of Gangnam—now world-famous thanks to Psy's hit song "Gangnam Style"—was named "Tehran-ro" in his honor.

Many Iranians don't know much about it, but after hearing my story, they give me a thumbs-up, saying it's truly touching. There are likely few other countries that would remember a gesture of goodwill for so long and consider it as precious as a name.

Amir's Lyft taxi carries me down a manicured, tree-lined road through Atherton, a Silicon Valley suburb with the highest median home price in the country—$12 million in ZIP code 94027. Here, homes on more than an acre of land are listed at the highest prices in the nation.

As we pass through a town where many Iranian royals and high-ranking officials fled after the collapse of the Pahlavi dynasty in 1979, the scene shifts to a working-class Hispanic neighborhood before I arrive at my destination: an auto detailing shop. My old Mercedes, which I dropped off in the morning for $180, waits for me, transformed after a full day of cleaning, including steam-cleaning the interior carpets. It looks like a new car. Two days ago, I spent $450 at a mechanic in the same neighborhood fixing an engine overheating issue caused by a leaky water pipe.

At the height of his popularity, Nam Jin, a patriotic singer from the Honam region of the country I deeply respect, proudly enlisted in the Marine Corps and risked his life. He even served in the Vietnam War in 1969 at 23. On the way back to the office, a song by Nam Jin softly echoes in my car. I hum along, *"Life is about getting drunk on an empty glass anyway; you fill my empty glass with the rest of my sorrows~."*

My Mercedes, my loyal companion for over 10 years, feels like a reflection of life itself. When I fix one thing, something else breaks down, and the annual repair costs feel like at least $1,500. Yet, I can't bring myself to part with it so easily.

What is life to me? It feels like quietly repairing and cherishing an old Mercedes—moving forward together without saying a word.

Reflection on My Vietnamese Friends

2019-08-10 (Sat)

"Oh my, you're almost drowning... Okay, let's try this."

If you do two dolphin kicks with your feet together and push the water hard backward with your arms, your face will naturally emerge from the water. Then, quickly inhale, pull both outstretched arms behind you above the water, and forcefully throw them forward while pushing your head back into the water. This way, you can perform a much more dynamic butterfly stroke.

The small Vietnamese woman who gave me this quick swimming tip was a local high school math teacher who had graduated from Stanford University's Graduate School of Education. I had met her at the pool a few months ago. I mentioned that I could manage freestyle and breaststroke, but the butterfly and backstroke were the most challenging. As I left the swim lane after my swim, she kindly observed me and offered coaching on the butterfly stroke.

Her name is 'Lam,' which sounds like 'sheep.' Whenever I meet her, I can't help but think of *The Silence of the Lambs*, the film featuring Jodie Foster's brilliant portrayal of FBI agent Starling and Anthony Hopkins' eerie, devilish performance as the infamous psychiatrist Hannibal Lecter. I always find it amusing to call her by the movie title, though her name doesn't have the silent "b" like 'lamb' in the movie.

After the fall of South Vietnam in late April 1975, hundreds of thousands of Vietnamese refugees fled their homeland on boats, drifting across the vast seas of South China. Many were rescued and lived in camps in places like Hong Kong before being dispersed to four regions with climates similar to Vietnam's: Los Angeles, Houston, New Orleans, and San Jose, thanks to the humanitarian efforts of the United States. Orange County's "Little Saigon" is the most well-known for its bustling commercial district, but San Jose has the largest Vietnamese population.

In the 1980s, as these refugees settled, Silicon Valley was booming with job opportunities. Today, the region is home to about 180,000 Vietnamese, making it the largest Vietnamese population outside of mainland Vietnam. The community has grown strong, giving rise to city council members and standing shoulder to shoulder with other immigrant groups, such as the Chinese, Japanese, and South Indian communities, all of which have long histories of immigration.

Another Vietnamese friend I met at the pool is Duc, whose name sounds similar to mine. He is a respectable software engineer in his mid-50s but carries a sadness he cannot hide. His only son, now in his mid-20s, suffers from mild mental retardation. Duc is always by his son's side, watching over him with concern and pity, whether they are swimming or not. Over the past 10 years, as a friend, I have come to know this naturally.

Duc shared that his entire family escaped just before the fall of South Vietnam in April 1975. He had heard from a relative working at the U.S. Embassy in Saigon that the war was turning unfavorable. About 20 days before the fall, a shocking event occurred: a South Vietnamese Air Force pilot flew an F-5 and dropped a bomb on the presidential palace, firing a machine gun with the intent to kill then-President Nguyen Van Thieu.

Duc followed his parents at just 12 years old, who could no longer delay their escape. His family boarded the last flight arranged by the U.S. Embassy in Saigon and made their way to the United States.

Reflecting on the situation on the Korean Peninsula today, I can't help but feel anxious that a similar shocking event could occur, leading to the country's collapse in an absurd manner and creating millions of refugees.

The current government's actions—pushing diplomacy with Japan to the brink, fueling an emotional anti-Japanese boycott, and some even invoking historical figures like Admiral Yi Sun-sin's 12 ships and the Donghak bamboo spear unit to stir confrontation—are concerning. As if that weren't enough, absurd curses are circulating about the Japanese archipelago sinking in a volcanic eruption.

It's painful to hear ominous warnings that Japan's economic retaliation could trigger a stock market crash, a sharp rise in the exchange rate, and even a second IMF financial crisis—disasters that would be devastating for Korea.

I hope the president of my homeland can wisely resolve this situation, understanding deeply that his most important duty is to govern safely so that the people can live in peace, enjoying the fruits of a prosperous economy. We must not allow Korea, the proud Asian tiger we built with blood, sweat, and tears over the past 50 years, to be destroyed.

Morning of Awakening

2019-09-14 (Sat)

"I'm too scared to buy a gun. I have this ominous feeling that I might shoot somebody someday."
"That's why I've made up my mind. I bought it to protect myself and my loved ones, but I'll never use it on myself unless it's necessary."

We had a conversation after seeing a friend's post about receiving his gun three days after ordering it. He mentioned that he only takes it out at the shooting range.

He's a Black man, three or four years younger than me, and we've been friends for over 15 years. About three years ago, his white gay husband, who was nearly 20 years older than him, passed away from a stroke, leaving him a house worth $1 million. He sold it, bought at least two homes in Las Vegas, where the cost of living is lower than in the San Francisco area, and relocated there.

He lived in Las Vegas for two years, where the famous slogan "What happens here, stays here" often played on TV commercials. He occasionally shares interesting posts about his work in Sacramento, which I quickly repost for my Korean community to see and earn points.

When I first met him, he was a top law firm in Palo Alto secretary and weighed 350 pounds. I was shocked when he shared that he couldn't lose weight despite his best efforts. About five years ago, as a last resort, he had gastric bypass surgery, which created a tiny 30 cc upper gastric pouch, directly connecting it to his small intestine, forcing him to eat less. Amazingly, he lost so much weight that he dropped to 220 pounds, reaching a weight similar to mine.

It might be a similar example, but I had this growing sense of anxiety: *If I buy a dashcam, I might end up in an accident that makes me need it.* Still, I couldn't resist and bought one about a month ago.

But... on the high-resolution dashcam screen, a perfectly healthy man is shown getting out of his car with a helpless expression. He looks up at the sky, sighs deeply, and grabs his head with both hands before turning toward the curb.

That man, sitting in front of the sobbing girl on the side of the road, was none other than me—meditating in resignation. It was as if I had been caught in a trap, causing an absurd accident without the chance to react.

I was feeling lost and had nowhere to go during the holiday. Still, I unexpectedly met a kind Japanese woman, the head of a Silicon Valley innovation Centre for a significant Japanese tech company, TOTO. She became a last-minute connection, and we spent the Labor Day holiday pleasantly—playing two rounds of golf and going on a hike. On my first day back at work, I happily sang along to the wonderful seasonal song *The Sound of September Coming* by Patty Kim, which a friend in Korea had uploaded for me when the accident suddenly happened.

I had just stopped at a red light, preparing to turn right after making sure no cars were coming from the left. Out of nowhere, a tiny Hispanic girl—who, unbelievably, was 19 years old—rode her bicycle into the crosswalk and crashed into my car.

It all played out in slow motion as if I were watching a movie: the girl falling off her bike, landing on the car's hood, and then sliding back down onto the roadway.

When I was a child growing up near the masonry, I played soccer several times a day with teams hastily organized in the neighborhood. Having continued running for over 40 years, I've become quite fit and have often boasted about my athletic ability.

When I played soccer during the company sports days at the bank I worked for in Korea, I was a left winger known for my agility and ability to use both feet, continuing to play well into my mid-30s. I had always prided myself on my athletic ability, so accepting this kind of accident was difficult. Not only was the girl shocked by the crash, but I also learned a humbling lesson: life shouldn't be taken so lightly.

Fortunately, the girl didn't appear to be seriously injured, aside from the shock. The police arrived quickly, along with a fire truck. After listening to my explanation and checking my vehicle registration and insurance certificate, they didn't issue any tickets besides a routine traffic accident report. They said, "You are free to go."

If you reflect on this kind of experience and drive more carefully in the future, the likelihood of a bigger accident decreases—it can be a blessing in disguise. While unexpected accidents may happen at varying frequencies, no one is exempt. That morning, you taught me a meaningful lesson: to live humbly and avoid arrogance in every moment.

Edelweiss

2019-10-19 (Sat)

Small and white, clean and bright
You look happy to meet me.
Blossom of snow
May you bloom and grow
Bloom and grow forever...
Edelweiss...
Bless my homeland forever...

Famous song Edelweiss in the Movie Sound of Music

In the lobby of the Palo Alto, a small concert was held for the first time in 18 years, as far as I know. When this song played as the final piece, the faces of the 10 or so members—young and old, fluent and not-so-fluent English speakers—lit up with happy smiles as they sang together.

The concert was organized by a group of friends who would meet almost every day at the pool and jacuzzi, which closed at 9:45 p.m., ending their day with friendly chats.

Mike, a CPA overseeing accounting at a major insurance brokerage firm, served as a Mormon missionary in Tokyo for two years in his early 20s. He could still speak basic Japanese, like "Oyasumi Nasai" (Good night!). Every Thursday afternoon, he flies his private Cessna from Palo Alto Airfield to his home near Sacramento to spend time with his family, returning on Sunday night.

Mike, a 67-year-old white man, played the first guitar, while James, of similar age, played the second. James's right leg, stiff from arthritis, could barely bend, and his face sometimes contorted in pain as he continued his decades-long work as a gardener, leaning on a cane to support his bad leg.

Mike kindly received my song request by email and

printed out the lyrics to the Beatles' *Ob-La-Di, Ob-La-Da* in large letters so the immigrant friends could sing along. While it was hard to follow the fast-paced lyrics, and my tongue was practically sweating, I confidently sang Edelweiss's final song without even needing to look at the lyrics.

After wrapping up the finale with a familiar song, we happily parted ways and headed home along the moonlit road.

Many Americans mistakenly believe that *Edelweiss* is the German national anthem, as it's frequently sung by Germans. However, the truth is that it was a hymn for German resistance fighters against Hitler's Nazis during World War II.

Edelweiss, a small yet beautiful flower, grows on steep limestone cliffs between 1,800 and 3,000 meters above sea level—higher than Mount Baekdu—so steep that even mountain goats cannot reach it. In the 19th century, it symbolized noble charm among the Alpine people. The name *Edelweiss* is German, and when translated into English, it means "precious white flower" or "noble white."

This precious Edelweiss flower is carefully preserved in my old photo album, along with a picture of a foreign girl wearing large black horn-rimmed glasses. The story goes back 44 years to when I was a freshman in high school. At that time, it was popular to have pen pals from other countries, but writing letters in English wasn't easy, so not many of my friends participated.

I gathered the courage to apply, and a student magazine sent me an address. That's how I began an international pen-pal friendship with a German girl named Iris. It was indescribably joyful to receive an airmail envelope with the red and blue *PAR AVION* border once a month.

One day, I opened the envelope from Germany that the postman handed me, and I was overcome with excitement. Inside was a single, well-dried white Edelweiss flower, attached to a black card the size of a business card, wrapped in plastic, and a photo of my pen pal, Iris. It was the first time in my life that I had received such a precious gift from a girl—and from a pen pal overseas. The gesture swept over my heart with great emotion, touching the soul of this crew-haircut high school student.

I wondered what kind of uniquely Korean gift I could send in return, so I went to a stamp shop in front of my school and had a wooden stamp made. I engraved her name in Korean, as it was pronounced, and sent it to Germany with a cute little red ink pad. Unfortunately, due to various pressures—worries about my studies and future—I couldn't continue our pen pal relationship, and it remains a regret to this day.

Reading an online dictionary's explanation that *Edelweiss*, also called the "Star of the Alps," is given as a symbol of love by locals, I slapped my forehead. *Wait...* Does that mean Iris sent me the Edelweiss as a confession of love 45 years ago? You idiot, how did you not realize that?

Smiling at the bright full moon, I send an unaddressed letter to her, who must be an elegant old lady somewhere in Germany by now, saying, *"I hope you are healthy and happy."*

Excitement At Dawn

2019-11-23 (Sat)

"Hey... I guess it does matter what time you go to bed." Adrian is a second-generation Chinese man in his early 40s, about my nephew's age, who handles global sourcing of core components like memory and camera modules at Apple. Richard, a Chinese man in his mid-50s who works in a different internet business division at Apple, laughed and chimed in.

After completing an intense Saturday aqua survival class with a Navy boot camp theme, we were catching our breath in the hot tub. Their reactions came when I asked if it was true that Tim Cook, Apple's CEO, wakes up at 3:45 every morning.

Surprisingly, he gets up so early, but I joked about Cook, saying, "How early must he go to bed if he's waking up at that hour?" After a good laugh, I asked if they knew there was a global business figure in Korea who was also famous for waking up early, and they both perked up, curious to know who it was.

I then told them the story of the late Hyundai Group founder Chung Ju-Yung, who couldn't stay in bed past 4 a.m. because he was too excited about the work he'd be doing that day—just 15 minutes later than Tim Cook.

Their curiosity deepened as I shared more about him.

In the summer of 1986, after being discharged as a lieutenant from Air Force Headquarters in Daebang-dong, Seoul, I started working at Korea Exchange Bank, which was located on the first and second floors of the Hyundai Group building. This building was constructed on the former site of Whimoon High School in Gye-dong, next to Biwon (meaning secret garden of the dynasty), which had relocated to Gangnam.

While managing international tasks such as letters of credit for exports and imports, as well as various bonds like construction bid bonds, advance payment refund bonds, and performance bonds, I gained a deeper understanding of Chairman Chung Ju-Yung and Hyundai Group's various global projects. The title of this essay is inspired by a touching collection of autobiographical essays about Chairman Chung, which I read repeatedly, highlighting each passage.

When I asked if they knew that the late Chairman Chung Ju-Yung—who founded global companies like Hyundai Motor, Hyundai Heavy Industries, Hyundai Construction, and Hynix—was an elementary school dropout, their curiosity grew. They joked that despite graduating from prestigious Stanford and Ivy League institutions like UPenn, they didn't feel very influential in Silicon Valley. They were referring to the fact that many of Silicon Valley's dominant founders were also dropouts.

Microsoft's Bill Gates and Facebook's Mark Zuckerberg dropped out of Harvard, Apple co-founder Steve Jobs left Reed College in Oregon, and Oracle's Larry Ellison dropped out of the University of Chicago.

So, who exactly was Chairman Chung Ju-young, who dropped out of elementary school? I continued the story. Born as the eldest son of a poor farmer in Tongcheon-ri, Asan-myeon, Gosung-gun, Gangwon-do—now part of North Korea—Chung Ju-young was a young man who dreamed of bigger things beyond the mundane life of helping with farming in the countryside.

In 1932, at 17, he stole the money his father had saved from selling their cow—then the family's most valuable asset—and ran to Seoul. My swimming friends, who were listening to my storytelling, looked at me with puzzled expressions as I recounted this.

His heartbroken father took the Gyeongwon Line local train to Seoul, a 12-hour journey, and eventually found his son attending a bookkeeping academy in Seosomun. He brought him back to their hometown after tearfully persuading him over a meal at a nearby gomtang, a Korean-style beef broth soup restaurant. But Chung Ju-young was determined—he ran away from home for the fourth time. He worked as a dockworker at Incheon Port before moving to Gyeongseong (Seoul) and getting a job as a rice deliveryman at a rice shop in Ahyeon-dong.

The rice shop owner recognized the sincerity and accounting skills of the young Chung Ju-young. Instead of passing the business to his son, who was more interested in women, he entrusted the rice shop to the 23-year-old Chung. From there, Chung took over an automobile repair shop, a cutting-edge industry at the time, and created numerous legends in Korea's economy. These included the construction of the Gyeongbu meaning Seoul -Busan Expressway in record time during the five-year economic development plan after the May 16 Revolution, the founding of Hyundai

Motor Company, building the world's largest shipyard on the white sands of Ulsan, and leading major overseas construction projects.

I continued my story to the point where Chairman Chung dramatically repaid his father for his youthful act of stealing money, running away, and driving a wedge into their relationship. In November 1998, he famously drove 1,000 cows across the Military Demarcation Line as a gift to North Korea. My friends pictured the spectacle of 1,000 cows crossing the border while I, recounting the tale, glanced up at the late autumn sky through the foggy window. Thanksgiving was approaching, and I couldn't help but reflect on the miraculous rise of the Republic of Korea.

Outside, a flock of geese flew in a perfect V formation, flapping their wings diligently as they followed their leader southward to warmer climates.

To My Beloved Sisters

2019-12-28 (Sat)

Ptosis? I glanced at my left eyelid in the rearview mirror on the way to the hospital and noticed it drooping. It seemed to be a side effect of rapidly losing 8 pounds over four days through a 60-hour fast—a weight I had slowly gained over the past year.

A few days ago, I had returned from a ten-day trip to my home country, the first in four years, and was already feeling off due to jet lag. To make things worse, a mix-up with my exam schedule forced me to fast twice, drinking only the prescribed liquid laxative. Yesterday, the side effects hit me hard—my head felt like it was going to split open, and I collapsed at my desk, fearing I might not make it through the day. After taking a deep nap for the first time in nearly 30 years, I barely recovered, leaving work early without even having lunch.

Next, I went to the ultra-modern Kaiser Hospital next to Apple's Spaceship campus in Cupertino for colonoscopy and endoscopy tests at the same time. After the procedure, still groggy from the anesthesia, my sister Lian—a Chinese woman from Shanghai whom I met in Silicon Valley—came to pick me up.

Lian is the wife of my best friend, Steve, a Danish-

American. She exudes a calmness typical of China's great culture and is, at heart, a warm and kind woman. The couple, married for about 30 years, used to run a grocery market in a shopping mall near Palo Alto. Steve founded the business in 1974 when he was in his early 20s, and after 45 successful years, they hit the jackpot when they sold the market to a developer for the shopping mall's redevelopment.

Sister Lian remembered my upcoming birthday when I checked in at the hospital, saying she would prepare a nice dinner for me when I turn 60 early next year. I can't express how much Steve and Lian mean to me, especially being alone here. They genuinely care about my business, love life, and other personal matters. They are like a real family, truly warm and supportive, in this foreign land.

Before Thanksgiving, I received an invitation from my nephew to attend his wedding in Busan at the age of 38. For a moment, I was torn. Should I delay closing a new VIP client deal and fly to Korea? What eventually pushed me to the airport, despite my hesitation, was a sense of duty—an invisible pull that I needed to be there in place of my brother, who passed away 10 years ago.

After a 14-hour connecting flight, I arrived at Gimhae International Airport in Busan. I rested for a day at my 66-year-old sister's apartment, where she lives alone, and the next day, I headed to the BEXCO wedding hall. When I showed up unexpectedly, my nephew, his new bride, and my sister-in-law—who married into the family about 40 years ago—were so surprised and overjoyed to see me. All the awkwardness I had felt vanished instantly.

Reuniting with relatives, I hadn't seen in decades quenched my long-held thirst for family connections. After the ceremony, we visited my younger sister's daughter's apartment near Haeundae New Town. We shared memories over bottle of makgeolli, a traditional rice wine and Pajeon, a green onion Pancake with my aunt, now in her 90s, and a retired elementary school teacher from Jinhae, my cousin, and my sisters. Laughter filled the room, and the joy of being together again eased the longing for the past.

As my immediate older sister, a former high school bully, told a string of hilarious stories that made me laugh out loud, my older sister said something tugging at my heart in passing. "If I had been as tenacious and vicious as our younger sister, I wouldn't have dropped out of high school, embarrassed about being unable to pay my tuition fee on time..."

My father worked as a teacher at a Japanese elementary school in Japan as a Korean. When Korea was liberated, he returned to Busan at 24. The business he started thrived for about 20 years but failed around 1964. My eldest sister, who was once raised like a princess in a luxury residential area, suddenly found herself living on the outskirts of Seoul, shocked by the drastic change in her environment. When I think of her life—so talented in art but unable to fully realize her beautiful dreams as she aged—it breaks my heart.

Also, my elementary school girlfriends, who traveled from Seoul with gifts to welcome me back home, and my lovely cousins, two or three years younger than me, threw a welcoming bottle of makgeolli, a traditional rice wine and Pajeon, a green onion Pancake party in Jeongdong, Seoul. They're all like sisters to me, and my affection for them runs deep.

To all my wonderful sisters, wherever you are on this planet, thank you for being so dear to me. Let's continue to live by the riverside, where our memories of the past shimmer like silver sand. In the bright new year of 2020, the year of the rat, I hope that all of my sisters find even greater happiness.

Cherishing Precious Moments and People

2020-02-01 (Sat)

When you live a hectic life, visiting Korea every year isn't easy. That's why I find myself talking about my trip at the end of last year—my first in four years—as if it were a big deal.

After returning from Korea, my biological rhythm changed, and due to fasting twice for medical examinations, I started going to the gym 30–40 minutes later than my usual 6:30 a.m. routine. Over the past month, I naturally saw friends who arrived later but missed the ones I used to see simultaneously. It briefly felt like they had moved to a different place. How sweet is the simple pleasure of lying in bed and telling yourself, "Just five more minutes," while lazily scrolling through your smartphone to catch up on what happened overnight?

But today, I jumped out of bed, thinking, *"This won't do!"* I got to the gym at my usual early hour, showered, and headed to the hot tub by the pool. To my surprise, Jenny, whom I hadn't seen in about a month, hurriedly followed me into the hot tub after finishing her swim.

"Where have you been?" We both asked the question at

the same time. Jenny, a medical doctor from Beijing, was the first to explain. At the end of last year, she quit her job as a research doctor at the Palo Alto VA Hospital, where she had worked for 25 years, to focus entirely on her new drug development startup.

She explained that while juggling two jobs had taken a toll on her mentally and physically, she now feels much more at ease, able to concentrate fully on her work.

Jenny, two or three years younger than me, is an accomplished person who came to the U.S. about 30 years ago as a Chinese government-sponsored international student and settled here. She's a graduate of a prestigious Chinese university. According to Jenny, China's four most prestigious universities are Beijing Medical University, Tsinghua University, Beijing University, and Fudan University in Shanghai. She graduated from Beijing Medical University and met her husband, a Beijing University graduate, during the national scholarship selection exam. They both came to the U.S. to study together.

Jenny says life is a series of endless worries, concerns, and choices. Though she hesitated a lot before quitting her full-time job, she now feels more confident and energized as she focuses on her business. While the burden of taking full responsibility for everything weighs on her, she feels capable of handling it. Next month, she's scheduled to go to New York to meet with people from an investment bank affiliated with JP Morgan to discuss attracting investment.

When Jenny asked, "Where have you been hiding, and what have you been up to?" I couldn't help but brag about my recent trip to Korea. I mentioned that I had a wonderful time celebrating my 60th birthday at a Japanese restaurant in Palo Alto run by a close client. She looked a bit disappointed and asked why I hadn't invited her, which made me apologetic.

At the party, my eldest son, who works at Samsung Electronics in Silicon Valley, and my younger son, a CPA, attended and served the guests diligently. My eldest son, who had been distant for a while, came with an awkward smile, placed candles on the birthday cake, and did his best to socialize with the guests. He stayed until the end, showing what a thoughtful son he is, and even gave me a generous check to help cover the party expenses.

My younger son, who works for a national real estate development company run by three Jewish partners in Hollywood, sent me a luxury brand tie as a gift—the first of its kind. He explained that he was too busy to attend my 60th birthday party, but I told him that a 60th birthday is a once-in-a-lifetime event. Without saying another word, he flew up to join us.

Both of my sons worked hard, serving and chatting with the 40 or so guests, all close friends of mine. My younger son, who had to work overtime, said his goodbyes to each guest before rushing to the airport. Watching them put in such effort warmed my heart.

At the party, one of the eldest guests, Mr. Cho, gave a congratulatory speech to my American friends in Palo Alto and then proposed a toast, praising my sons for growing up well. I snuck up to my boys, pretended to whisper in their ears, and surprised them with a kiss on the cheek.

Oh! My proud sons, I love you so much! Their faces, sharing in the happiest moment of their father's life, reflected a gentle wave of happiness.

When the joyful 60-year-old father began to sing a song, his foreign friends joined in with shoulder dances, and the Koreans chimed in with the chorus:

"~Remote island village on the sea where the eglantine flowers bloom and fall~"

Until the Heaven Calls Us

2020-03-07 (Sat)

"Lieutenant Kim!" A familiar, welcoming voice greeted me over the phone.

It was already 30 years ago. I was working on a special team for the Hyundai Group on the second floor of the Korea Exchange Bank in Gye-dong, Jongno-gu, reviewing thick documents related to FX validation under the Foreign Exchange Transaction Act. It was unusual for a locked-in jail prisoner to call a bank branch, especially one that was not directly involved in trading.

The voice belonged to Colonel Kang Yong-lin, who had served as the Air Force attaché at the Republic of China Embassy in Myeongdong, Seoul, until early 1989. He was a tall, slender, 6-foot-tall elite fighter pilot who had become a close friend when I worked as an attaché liaison officer at the ROK Air Force Headquarters in Daebang-dong. Kang was a standout pilot in the Taiwanese Air Force, so when I heard he was returning to Taiwan after completing his three-year term, I often imagined him rising through the ranks to become the Air Force Chief of Staff, given his kind personality and excellent skills as a fighter pilot.

I was somewhat puzzled when I later learned that he had been discharged shortly after returning to Taiwan and had become a pilot for a commercial airline. During our time together in military diplomacy, we were always very polite to one another, but I felt that he genuinely cared for me. After I was discharged, as a rookie in my new career, I was invited to his private residence at the now-demolished Namsan Foreigner Apartment in Hannam-dong. I still remember the luxury of being treated to Chinese delicacies such as bird's nest soup and shark's fin, accompanied by high-quality liquor, with my eldest child in tow, who had just turned one.

He was about thirteen years older than me, like my eldest brother, and he was a very polite gentleman with the air of a wonderful person from a great nation. His wife, who had taken a leave of absence from teaching commerce at a high school in Hsinchu, an industrial city south of Taipei, and came to Korea with him, would bring out Oolong tea, a famous Chinese tea after meals and chat while drinking it together. Then, his twelve-year-old daughter, who had finished her homework at an international school, would come out in a pretty dress and sit at the piano, and his nine-year-old son would come out with a violin on his shoulder and play a wonderful duet for us.

At the time, I was newly married and living in a single room in Ssangmun-dong, Kkotdongne (a neighbor full of flowers), near Duksung Women's University in Ui-dong, Seoul. My dream was to be recognized at work, become a manager, and then be assigned to an overseas branch. We worked hard to achieve this goal, and as we watched the affluent daily lives of diplomats' families unfold before our eyes, we felt envious of such a home-sweet home, feeling that there was no other home like it.

I also respected him very much and got along well with

him, and that relationship continued even after we left the military and entered society. Whenever he stopped at Gimpo on his Boeing plane for China Airlines, he would call me to say hello, and at the end of the year, he would send me a Christmas card before anyone else. Every time, I would make excuses that I was busy, and I would hurriedly reply for several years.

Then, in 1997, the IMF financial crisis hit. Determined to be the first to send a card that year, I went to the Myeongdong Central Post Office, chose a beautiful card, and sent it. I felt satisfied for the first time in a while, but for some reason, I never heard back from him.

The following year, still without a word, I visited the Taiwanese representative office, which had moved to Doryeom-dong in Gwanghwamun, and asked a Chinese employee about his well-being. With a meaningful expression, he gave me a short, vague answer: "He is not here now," and refused to say more.

What did that even mean? An ominous feeling settled in my gut as if something terrible had happened. Twenty years after the incident, I was shocked to hear the details from a Taiwanese engineer friend I had met in Silicon Valley.

It was an unbelievable story. In 1998, the runway suddenly appeared in the fog while attempting to land at Taipei Chiang Kai-shek Airport, flying an Airbus A300 from Bali, Indonesia. As he tried to gain altitude rapidly, the plane's tail struck the runway, igniting a fire. The plane crashed into a nearby residential area, and all 203 people on board tragically lost their lives.

At that time, many high-ranking government officials, including the governor of Taiwan's central bank, who had attended the IMF annual meeting, were on board the plane. Their deaths sent shockwaves through Taiwan. *Oh my gosh, I remember now.* That incident had been reported in the foreign media. I closed my eyes briefly, clasped my hands together, and prayed for his peace in heaven.

I have experienced a few other cases where I could never associate the person with the darkness of death, but now the Grim Reaper of Coronavirus seems to be circling us. Did the gunfire from Mia-ri during the Korean War make the residents of Donam-dong this anxious? It's hard to say. Until June, when a vaccine is expected, all we can do is diligently wash our hands, maintain personal hygiene, and remain true to ourselves.

Chapter 6

A Star Shining at Night

The Poster at Kelowna

2020-04-11 (Sat)

The moment I saw it, goosebumps covered my skin. The bold, urgent text read:

"To prevent the spread of infection, all schools, churches, theaters, cinemas, billiard halls, and other entertainment venues, public or private, are closed until further notice. All gatherings of more than 10 people are prohibited. - Mayor Sutherland."

As of April 10, the coronavirus pandemic had infected nearly 1.6 million people worldwide, claiming over 95,000 lives. Yet this proclamation wasn't from recent times—it was from a poster displayed in Kelowna, a city near Vancouver, Canada, on November 7, 1918, just days before the end of World War I, more than 100 years ago. It was a desperate attempt to contain the horrific Spanish flu, which infected 500 million people and claimed tens of millions of lives.

After a century of extraordinary scientific advancements, humanity has journeyed from the moon to Mars and beyond. Yet, in facing a modern pandemic, our fragility seems just as pronounced as it was in 1918. What progress did we truly make to remain so vulnerable in the face of another global health crisis?

Today, every corner of the globe is linked through high-speed 5G networks. We stand on the threshold of the 5th Industrial Revolution, driven by groundbreaking advancements in the Internet of Things (IoT), artificial intelligence, deep learning, cloud computing, and self-driving vehicles.

Medical technology, too, has made remarkable strides. Once considered a death sentence, AIDS is now a manageable chronic condition, and precision radiation therapy for cancer targets only affected areas, sparing surrounding organs from harmful side effects. Optimistic forecasts once claimed that humans might live to 120 years, sparking debates on whether such longevity, without sufficient resources, was a true blessing. Then, abruptly, the COVID-19 pandemic hit—a disaster eerily reminiscent of the Spanish flu from a century ago.

For all the difficulties of earthly life, few would readily choose death over life. And yet, in the world's most powerful nation, with its unmatched military might and technological prowess, the lack of preparation was staggering. By April 10, the U.S. was grappling with nearly 490,000 confirmed COVID-19 cases and 18,000 deaths—holding the grim record of the highest infection and mortality rate worldwide. This pandemic, like that of 1918, is a harsh reminder of our shared vulnerability in the face of such an invisible, sweeping force.

The unfolding tragedy, particularly in New York, is nothing short of a catastrophic collapse of the medical system. It's shocking—and humbling—to witness the United States, a nation that prides itself on its world-class status, facing such a crisis unprepared and seemingly helpless.

In our own community, the heartbreaking news has arrived: a 17-year-old high school student, full of youthful resilience, has succumbed to the virus. Now, having joined the ranks of seniors, I feel a sharp chill whenever I hear of such losses. It's as if death, shrouded in a dark hood, stalks this battlefield of illness with a net, and I lie low, hoping to avoid its reach—like a flounder pressed against the floor of a water tank in a live fish restaurant, eyes wide open, silently watching.

Yet amid this grim and roaring "Third World War" against a virus, a different force emerges: a spirit of kindness and selfless concern. In these bleakest of times, compassion becomes a bright lotus rising from the mud, illuminating our world. From checking in on one another to generously sharing masks, these acts of solidarity remind us that even in life's darkest corners, humanity has the power to shine.

Though we may not have had much in the bank, life was rich with warmth as long as we were surrounded by kind-hearted people. If tomorrow brings an untimely end, a casualty of this pandemic, there's little we can do to prevent it. But before that time comes, let's take a moment to call our loved ones, to hear each other's voices and express our gratitude for sharing this beautiful world together. Let's hold on as long as we can—and live through this, together.

A Guest from the Rambla

2020-05-16 (Sat)

"I'm sorry. In these uncertain times, a 10-year lease just isn't possible. Three years is the best I can offer."

Back in late February, as Italy saw a devastating surge in coronavirus cases and deaths, and Spain began to follow suit, I found myself working closely with two Italian partners. Alfredo, a chef in his early 40s, has run a highly acclaimed restaurant on Barcelona's renowned Rambla for a decade. Nestled among iconic sights like Gaudí's cathedral and the Barcelona FC stadium, where Messi's six-time Ballon d'Or-winning magic plays out, it's a restaurant with an incredible atmosphere and reputation. On weekends, Alfredo would sometimes catch Messi's artistry on the field, leaving me more than a bit envious.

Alongside him was Luigi, a savvy investor with an MBA from U.C. Berkeley, who shared an office with me. Together, they had a vision of opening a second location in downtown Palo Alto, right at Stanford University's main gate—a prime spot in Silicon Valley. We quickly dismissed other popular locations in San Francisco, focused on Palo Alto, and scouted sites without delay.

Then, without warning, the "shelter in place" (SIP) order

was announced, bringing everything to a halt. Just as plans were coming together, the world around us stopped.

Feeling dejected, Alfredo asked me to investigate one of the lease options I had suggested before he returned indefinitely to Barcelona. He'd been negotiating with an American landlord, but after two months of painfully slow responses, he finally received a disappointing "no."

Working closely with business partners from Italy and Spain—countries hit hardest by the pandemic in Europe—was a bit ironic. Yet, I didn't hesitate or second-guess. We left things to chance, met frequently without masks, and bonded over authentic Italian pizza and beer. Together, I worked tirelessly with Alfredo and Luigi, who were young enough to be my nephews, and now, I can't help but feel a sense of regret for them.

For property owners eager to sell at a premium to buyers with redevelopment plans, there's little incentive to commit to a 10-year lease, even for an acclaimed restaurant brand's second location. Yet, from Alfredo's and Luigi's perspective, establishing a high-end restaurant in such a prime spot demands a hefty initial investment—and a guaranteed lease of at least a decade to offset it. Despite the pandemic's chilling grip, projects like this are progressing ever so slowly, like fish gliding beneath a thick layer of ice in the bitter, unmoving cold of the city.

Last Saturday, I took a 13-kilometer walk to the beach with a Chinese engineer female friend who works at RAMBUS, a global Silicon Valley tech firm with a stronghold in memory semiconductor patents. During a time when economic stress is at an all-time high, Samsung Electronics, Korea's pride, announced some good news—meeting Wall Street's first-quarter earnings expectations. My friend mentioned that the outlook at RAMBUS was cautiously optimistic, thanks to steady chip orders from TSMC in Taiwan, which supplies Samsung and SK Hynix.

As the Shelter-In-Place stretches into its third month, I've found that my anxiety over COVID-19 has eased—I'm stronger now, less worried about when or if the virus might find me. My workload and wallet may be lighter, but the silver lining is real. My gym has been closed for ages, so I'm sleeping in for the first time in years. I wake up around 8, shower, do a set of deep squats and push-ups, and drive over to McDonald's to grab coffee at the curbside. After a quiet walk along the coast, I settle down in front of my computer, checking the status of my SBA emergency fund application, singing along to my favorite tunes, and killing time on social media. When evening comes, I head out for another long walk to hit my 14,000-step goal for the day.

The other day, I looked in the mirror and barely recognized the long-haired senior single guy staring back at me. He asked if maybe it was time to swing by Lisa's Vietnamese hair salon by Costco.

The Happy Sound

2020-06-20 (Sat)

"Miss Camelia, waiting again today~."

Looking back now, it's almost amusing, but in the 1970s, there was a time when the state monitored personal expression. Though the measures weren't precisely hostile, they were part of a broader societal push. Korea was emerging from centuries of poverty, energized by a five-year economic development plan, achieving world-leading growth rates similar to China's in more recent times. You could hear the familiar calls of street vendors in the alleys of hillside poor neighbors like Donam-dong, Seoul—"Sell your hair"—and women, hoping to save on salon trips, would let these vendors trim their long hair. They sold the cut hair to make wigs, earning some pocket money to buy their children small items like pencils or slippers.

The government at that time worried about young people falling into decadence, believing hedonism might weaken their drive to work for the country's progress. Police were deployed to measure hair covering the ears or skirts above the knee, wielding 30-centimeter rulers to ensure modesty. Those who didn't comply were sometimes lined up along the roadside, and even sure "decadent" or Japanese-influenced songs were banned from public airwaves. It was a strict era, but it also held a unique kind of charm, with a sense of purpose deeply woven into everyday life.

This is my morning walk along the peaceful shoreline beside Google Campus. Under soft white clouds, a dozen pelicans float on the water, happily feasting on their morning catch, beaks lifted high. Today's soundtrack is *Miss Camelia*, a version by the young Korean traditional music prodigy Song So-hee, who has been rarely seen lately. As I hummed along with her powerful YouTube rendition, a particular line—*"I feel so much pain without you as like my heart is cut out~"*—sent chills down my spine. When I got home, I decided to play the original song by Lee Mi-ja, recorded myself singing along in a calm voice, and uploaded it to YouTube and Facebook. To my surprise, 25 people clicked on it! It's astonishing that this heartbreakingly beautiful song was banned for so long, labeled as "Japanese."

It makes me wonder—what must it have been like for Koreans, who, by nature, are so spirited they can't help but dance even without music? Now, with the lockdown keeping us from seeing those we love, it's no surprise a friend in Sausalito recently joked about wanting to bang his head against the wall. Without music to lift our spirits, the isolation would be unbearable. Even now, I can vividly recall the joyful sounds of music from my childhood, the melodies that brought color to our world as soon as I was old enough to feel my five senses.

When liberation came in 1945, my father left his job as an elementary school teacher in Tokyo, Japan, and returned to Busan, S. Korea on a ship crossing the Genkai Strait. Back in Korea, he built a modest fortune through a UN military supply business. Some years later, in Gwangdaehyeon, Gimhae-up, a two-car train bound for Masan would pass by, and the sweet scent of tangerines filled the air. My dad bought a 5000-pyeong (approximately 4-acre) rice paddy as a pastime hobby farm for my grandmother, who was in her 60s at the time.

At just three years old, I would hold tightly to her hand at the Choryang Intercity Bus Terminal, determined not to let go, as we boarded the bus to Gimhae where the farm was. We would stay there for months, my small hand in hers as we enjoyed the peaceful rhythm of farm life.

My grandmother, seated nearby, would fill her metal pipe with finely powdered tobacco stored in a small square wooden grain-measuring container—square container filled with powder tobacco. Then she would take the powder to put into the small metal head of the long, wooden tobacco pipe. She would then ignite the fire using a match stick by striking it to the matching pad surrounding the matchbox to smoke tobacco.

Once she was done smoking, my grandmother struck the metal end of the pipe to the bronze ashtray two times to empty the ash from the pipe, creating a distinct two-strike rhythm that echoed softly around her.

On a made-in-Japan radio by the porch, the sounds of American light music like Washington Square and Park Jae-ran's hit, At the Southern Vills over the Hill, played alternately in the background. A candy vendor would pass by on the embankment behind the house, clicking his scissors to the rhythm to announce that he was coming.

Later, after my father's business failed, our family moved to an unfamiliar hillside village in Donam-dong, Seoul. Before starting elementary school, I was teased by Chun-ok, the girl from up the hill, for speaking in a Gyeongsang dialect. Then, in 4th grade, our class was selected as an ensemble class, and each student was assigned an instrument. I was given a melodica, and after practicing intensely in music class for months, I even participated in an ensemble competition at Sungin Elementary School in Jongam-dong. But as school progressed, music drifted out of reach, pushed aside by Korean, English, and math.

In 2001, while waiting for my H1-B visa to the U.S., I briefly rekindled that dream by taking three months of piano lessons at a children's academy in Bundang, a new town south of Seoul. Now, ironically, the pandemic has gifted me enough free time to continue where I left off. I ordered a 61-key keyboard online and, for the first time in nearly 20 years, began learning piano again—this time with lessons from an American YouTuber. Night after night, I've practiced, and now I can play the basic chords of C, D, F, G, and Am with both hands, even with my eyes closed.

When self-quarantine lifts in July, I hope I'll be able to play and sing Stephen Foster's *Beautiful Dreamer* with grace.

On a Starry Starry Night

2020-07-25 (Sat)

The sunset just before the sun dips below the horizon, struggling to linger a moment longer, is truly breathtaking. An hour or so after sunset, the darkening sky over the Palo Alto Baylands of San Francisco Bay in Northern California takes on a quiet beauty, with a faint red glow rising from its depths.

Now, here I am on a deserted shoreline at night, my heart fluttering with the excitement of a young boy, eager to witness a guest that has returned to our night sky after an eternity. The tide has come in, covering the tidal flats once exposed during the day. Black waves ripple here and there, reflecting moonlight across the quiet shoreline, and only the distant chorus of insects breaks the silence.

This is the story of Comet Neowise. The most famous comet to approach Earth is Halley's Comet, which graces us every 75 years. I still vividly recall the global excitement when it neared Earth in 1986, before our children were even born. Recently, I saw a photograph of Comet NEOWISE taken at dawn on the shores of a lake near Mount Shasta, a striking dormant volcano near the Oregon border. In the image, the comet's long tail stretched across the lake, its reflection mirrored perfectly on the still water. The sight was so captivating, I can only hope to see it with my own eyes tonight.

Drawn by a soft murmur in the darkness, I found a pair of amateur astronomers setting up a telescope on a tripod and holding an antique-looking scope that seemed straight out of the Soviet era, both aiming to spot the comet. I asked if they had found it yet. They pointed above the middle tree of three in the park, roughly at the same height as the treetop, in the direction of the sunset. But no matter how hard I squinted and searched, I couldn't catch a glimpse of it.

It was already 10 p.m., and the sodium lamps across the East Bay cast a hazy glow, making it harder to see the stars. The sky wasn't completely dark due to the interfering lights, and I quickly regretted not bringing even a small telescope. At least binoculars would have been necessary to see anything clearly. At any other time, I might have joked about sneaking a peek through someone else's telescope, but with COVID-19 and social distancing, that idea seemed far-fetched.

One of the guys, engrossed in the comet through his telescope, kindly pointed out Venus and Jupiter's locations to me, but I could only spot the Big Dipper and Polaris, the bright star at the end of its handle. Finding the other stars of our solar system among the vast night sky was impossible for me without any equipment.

About seven years ago, I had a rare chance to view our solar system's stars up close through an astronomical telescope. Foothill College, with its beautiful, spacious campus rivaling many four-year universities in S. Korea, had announced a community stargazing event, and I joined. The memory of that experience still lingers, as vivid as the stars themselves.

Following the professor's outstretched finger, I spotted the tiny, star-like space station gliding across the night sky from west to east. Then, when it was my turn, I eagerly peered through the long telescope the professor had carefully aimed. And there it was—Saturn, with its stunning rings on full display. The professor's explanation resonated: because the Earth rotates eastward, celestial bodies appear to move, and without continuous adjustment, a manual telescope can easily lose track. Saturn, the second-largest planet in our solar system after Jupiter, looked as small as a grain of rice, yet the thrill of seeing it firsthand was unforgettable.

During this long COVID-19 separation, alumni friends and acquaintances I haven't seen in nearly six months are reconnecting and sharing news of Comet NEOWISE, a comet that graces Earth's skies only every 6,800 years. Through KakaoTalk, we exchange observation experiences and comet updates, staying close despite the distance. In a way, it's these connections—brighter than any comet—that help us endure this isolating time, bringing a little wonder and warmth to our lives.

Memories of Geumjandi Square

2020-08-29 (Sat)

It's been years since I was last up at 3:30 a.m. studying. Recently, I took on a new venture and became an insurance agency owner. Now, I have to complete seven subjects through self-study, but after finishing just one, I mistakenly thought I was done. Now I'm hurriedly catching up on the assignments I missed, realizing it was a mistake to ignore all those emails. Looking back, I see that I've always worked hard at studying—though, like many, my efforts didn't always yield stellar results.

Back in January 1978, as a young bachelor, I started working tirelessly at the Central Bank of Korea. After a year on the accounting team in the international finance department, I had my first experience on the front line, meeting employees from major commercial banks, like the Korean Exchange Bank and Chohung Bank, every day at the counter. These banks provided export financing—known as "negotiation"—for medium to large sized trading companies, including industry giants like Samsung, Daewoo, and Hyundai. These firms, driven by the government's export push, were shipping everything from sweaters and wigs to enamelware and machinery abroad. They'd bring their export bills of exchange, secured as debt, to the central bank, use them as collateral, and receive a rediscount. It was a time of intense learning and growth, shaping my early career in ways I'm still grateful for today.

My job was to provide foreign currency liquidity to banks in the form of rediscounts, ensuring they could continue financing export companies. Around 4:30 p.m., after a busy day, I'd meet my high school friend Gyu-hwan, who worked in the IT department, at the cafeteria for a bowl of *Jajangmyeon (famous Korean black noodles)* before we headed to school together.

Each day, I never had a chance to leisurely sit on the beautiful Geumjandi Square—Geumjandi means Manila Grass in Korean—because I had such a tight daily schedule, like an early morning language course at academies, daily work before I went to evening college, and then self-study at the library until midnight. I took the No 8 city bus that runs to the Ui-dong terminal from the Taepyeong-ro bus stop. The bus passed the stone wall road along Biwon (a Dynasty's Secret Garden) and Chaggyeong-gung palace on my way to the Myeongnyun-dong campus.

It was known as S' University because many students entered after they failed to get admitted to the top SNU, Seoul National University. I'd arrive in time for my first class at 6 p.m., feeling alert. But by the second class, the *Jajangmyeon (famous Korean black noodles)* would start to sit heavily, and I'd stifle yawns, pinching my thighs or poking them with a ballpoint pen to stay awake. After classes, from 9 p.m. to midnight, I'd study in the law school library, and then the following day, I'd head to an academy to learn German or Japanese before going to work by 7 a.m. How tough those days must have been! Yet, I never felt it at the time.

On weekends, I'd visit my childhood friend Ki-cheol, a

transfer student from Yeosu, and his mother would serve us delicious Yeosu-style eel soup, proudly cooking for her son's friend. I'd barely get a bowl down before falling fast asleep, too tired even to talk. When I woke up, Ki-cheol would look at me, half-amused, half-annoyed, asking if I came over to sleep or to hang out. It was only then that I realized just how much my body was begging for rest.

My father had been ill for four years by the time I entered high school. Sensing the candle of life flickering, I would come home at midnight, exhausted, hoping for a heart-to-heart with my dad. He asked if I could come home a bit earlier, but I stubbornly refused, insisting that I needed every spare moment to study. When I did not have enough time to study at the library, he sadly passed away at such an early stage of his life. It remains one of the deepest regrets of my life, until his passing at just 58 from heart valve disease—a condition that is now easily treatable.

Despite his weakening health, he tirelessly put his Smith Corona typewriter to work, sending letters to foreign buyers with prices for aluminum pots, glassware, sweaters, and agar agar.

When we received an export letter of credit (L/C) from buyers in places like Saudi Arabia or the U.S., My dad coordinated with the company to ensure on-time shipments and handled negotiations at the bank. Those were celebratory days, where a successful deal meant a nice dinner and, sometimes, the chance to catch up on overdue tuition. However, in the spring of my sophomore year, when I was only 19, my father passed away unexpectedly, leaving a profound emptiness.

After his passing, I was transferred to the bank's Archive department, where I spent two years working as a reporter, proofreader, and editor for the in-house magazine *Bank of Korea News*. Once a month, I wrote articles on local branches spread across Korea's eight provinces. Eventually, I left the bank to focus on my studies, paying for my senior-year tuition with the severance pay I received. For months, I studied intensely in Ui-dong, Seoul and Hasangok-ri, Gwangju-up, and Gyeonggi-do, clocking in nearly 15 hours a day—the most focused study period of my life. However, with no immediate results, I could no longer delay my military service, so I applied for an Air Force officer in February 1983.

After discharge, and before my immigration in January 2002, I worked as a branch manager for Daewoo Group in front of Seoul Station. Later, I received a job offer from a Korean American bank in Silicon Valley, where I worked for three years before deciding to pursue my own business. I studied diligently for the real estate broker exam, spending three months at the Stanford Library with packed lunches, and passed on my first attempt. That was my last intense study experience, nearly 14 years ago.

They say learning is a lifelong journey, but perhaps this might be the final chapter where such rigorous study is required.

Hello, Mr. Hargrove!

2020-10-03 (Sat)

"Oh, God!" I leaped out of bed, heart pounding. Rushing to the kitchen, I was met with a terrifying sight: the pan was ablaze, smoke billowing into the air. Frantically, I turned off the gas and poured cold water into the smoking, red-hot pot. Sunday afternoon hadn't gone as planned—I usually prioritize a walk along Shoreline, but my mechanic had the car. Instead, I'd been chatting in bed with a friend when the smell of scorched cabbage hit my nose. I dreaded the thought of the smoke alarm going off, forcing me to clamber onto a chair to reset it. At least I could still smell; I suppose that's a good sign for my health in these COVID-19 times.

My conversation partner was Mr. Hargrove, a 67-year-old Marine veteran from Vancouver who served in Vietnam. He's a fan of Korean culture and often shares pictures and articles he thinks I'd enjoy. Recently, he sent me a photo of Cheomseongdae (a thousand-year-old observatory during the Silla Dynasty) with a friendly message. Our chats cover everything from everyday life to broader topics, spanning borders and echoing our shared Pacific Time Zone. My phone has been especially busy with ding~ding notifications from him lately.

Reflecting on my life, I've always focused on living

responsibly, steering clear of protests and anti-government activities. But I've changed over the past few years, deeply disillusioned by the current Korean government's divisive actions. False accusations surrounding a tragic maritime accident, the impeachment of a former female president, detainment of political opponents, deteriorating relations with Japan, and the dismantling of the nuclear power sector—it's been troubling to watch. Then there's the employment crisis stemming from policies affecting small businesses and the diplomatic submissiveness toward North Korea and China. I've been temporarily speechless and incapacitated by a sudden onslaught of absurdity. My mind seems to have taken a break.

Mr. Hargrove served in the Vietnam War as a U.S. Marine. After returning to Canada, he continued his service in a civilian capacity, contributing to the Canadian Marine Corps strength enhancement project as an expert. A dual citizen with a political leaning toward the U.S. Republican Party, he's a nature enthusiast who volunteers at a botanical garden on weekends. After hours of hard work, he enjoys tea time with the other volunteers, which sometimes even leads to a date.

He mentioned that he was already aware of Korea's current political and economic upheavals and fully understood my frustrations. Reassuringly, he reminded me that Korea is now seen as "a developed country recognized globally for its hard-won achievements" and applauded its impressive standing as the sixth-largest industrial producer in the world, following only China, the U.S., Japan, Germany, and India. This success, he said, is the result of fifty years of hard work—the Miracle on the Han River—and shouldn't be erased overnight.

These days, my meals consist of little more than a few

pieces of kimchi as my only vegetable. My mornings have become a struggle, and this past week, I was shocked to find blood in the toilet, possibly due to hemorrhoids or a change in my iron supplement. This symptom shows up every few months, but it's been more severe this time. My body is working overtime to replenish the lost blood, and I feel a constant, subtle fatigue from the strain on my hematopoietic stem cells. I can't help but worry that I might collapse from anemia even before the threat of the coronavirus.

Earlier this year, I had a double gastrointestinal endoscopy and colonoscopy, which thankfully showed no signs of colon cancer or other issues. Given that, my suspicions turned to a lack of fiber, likely due to my diet, combined with the stress of long hours studying for a new business venture. Determined to improve my diet, I bought a whole cabbage, knowing its tender leaves develop a natural sweetness when cooked. I nearly scorched the pot in the process, but it reminded me that more vegetables are probably the best path forward— Unfortunately, a tonic made from a thousand-year-old ginseng root probably won't grant you immortality.

Despite the COVID-19 pandemic, Chuseok, Korea's biggest holiday, has arrived as it does each year. Recently, we heard heartening news from Korea: a performance by legendary singer Na Hoon-a reached the highest viewership rating in Korean broadcast history, bringing a sense of comfort to those traveling home. For those of us in the U.S., this Chuseok feels especially nostalgic. Tonight, we plan a moonlit walk along the ocean, gazing at the bright full moon and feeling that much closer to home.

The Owl of the Shoreline

2020-11-07 (Sat)

Perhaps it's the sleeplessness after watching the U.S. presidential election broadcast through the night, or maybe it's the sudden dip to a chilly 47 degrees, but the usually lively shoreline promenade I walk every day is unusually quiet. For the past seven months, I've replaced my gym routine with a steadfast 10-kilometer walk every morning and evening, rain or shine. The parking lot at Shoreline Golf Course—about the halfway mark of my morning route—is completely empty, absent of golfers' cars.

Just a few steps from the trail, I passed the burrow of the Burrowing Owl, a rare and protected bird in these parts, known for its squirrel-like burrows amid the grassy terrain. Nearby, Francisco, a retired Mexican civil servant in his late 60s whom I had seen almost daily until a month ago, waved cheerfully and greeted me. His regular seaside walks are a constant, always with the same solemn expression, wearing his signature light green fleece jacket, gray pants, and thick black horn-rimmed glasses.

A bit later, I encountered Angelina, a woman who appeared to be around my age. After a couple of months of merely acknowledging each other with nods, I finally mustered the courage to initiate a greeting. With her Eastern European accent and the subtle scent of lavender, she's become a familiar figure. Yesterday and today, our paths have crossed, and this morning, she seemed intrigued by my steaming McDonald's coffee, commenting, "That looks delicious."

The U.S. presidential election, a global spectacle that occurs every four years, kept the world on edge all night. As billions across various countries followed the vote count, dawn finally broke. This was the 46th U.S. presidential election and my first as a U.S. citizen, having been naturalized just a year ago. I even contributed about $300 to the Trump campaign over three installments, receiving a dark blue shirt with a beautifully embroidered American flag in return.

I watched the unfolding results with intense interest, hoping they'd align with my predictions. As reports came in showing Trump performing unexpectedly well in key swing states like Florida and Pennsylvania, my enthusiasm rose. It almost felt as if I were in the race myself, eagerly relaying vote-count updates to friends and acquaintances in Korea.

Full of energy, I headed to the kitchen, selecting a Yukgaejang, a spicy Korean beef stew packet, and a can of perilla leaf salad that my 67-year-old sister from Gimhae had lovingly sent. I whipped up a delicious bibimbap with fresh market vegetables, two fried eggs, gochujang, and sesame oil, savoring it with the warm Yukgaejang and two glasses of eggnog—a treat I always indulge in as the year draws to a close. Satisfied, I went to bed around 11 p.m., feeling content.

But what awaited me in the morning? They say history is made at night, and indeed, it felt that way as I caught the news before my morning walk. Overnight, a deluge of mail-in ballots in Michigan created a startling shift—130,000 votes for Biden to zero for Trump, flipping the outcome entirely.

While the final results are still pending, networks like CNN, which has been notably critical of Trump, predicted Biden's win with over a 90% probability. Yet, the actual election has proven far more unpredictable, with Biden only managing to clinch the lead at the last moment. Regardless of who ultimately wins, these outlets are likely to face scrutiny for their reporting, as once again, the objectivity and accuracy expected from the media seem compromised in favor of projecting their preferences rather than facts.

Watching this immense democratic process, I can't help but question the resilience of America's election system, which invests nearly a full year—about 25% of a presidential term—in uncertainty every four years. Can it remain competitive in the face of China's growing power under Xi Jinping's authoritarian, lifelong leadership? Without Trump, I worry America may be left vulnerable to China's unrelenting strategies. And as a concerned citizen, I find myself wondering, what should I do?

Only Sadness Remains

2020-12-12 (Sat)

"Half a tank. Time to refuel." Today, I'm on a three-hour business trip to Sacramento, the state capital, where gold was famously discovered in 1849 along the Russian River, sparking the California Gold Rush. As I start the car, I glance at the gas gauge on the dashboard and can't help but smile—I bought this new car with the $8,000 signing bonus I received when I took on an additional role as the owner of a Farmers Insurance Agency last October. Sacramento, where a single phone call last year led to three successful deals, has come to feel like a lucky city.

I search for the Costco gas station in Vacaville, roughly the halfway point, and enter it into the navigation. Instead of taking the expected route east through Pleasanton, it directs me to head north on Freeway 101, past San Francisco Airport, through downtown, across the Bay Bridge, and past Berkeley.

Will Sacramento bring more good fortune this time? As I drive, I play a soothing YouTube playlist of Yu Ik-jong's songs, gradually turning up the volume and singing along, *"Our unforgettable love, only sadness remains in this heart..."*

About 30 minutes later, I passed through Millbrae, where my senior Nam—13 years my senior from college and a dear friend—once had his office near San Francisco Airport. A wave of loss washes over me; Nam, who was like a kind older brother, someone I could share my thoughts and worries with, especially over the past 7-8 years of my 20-year journey in the San Francisco Bay Area, is no longer with us. He was my mentor, my confidant, and, in many ways, my greatest supporter.

According to his own account, when he first arrived in the United States, reluctantly and at the invitation of his wife's family about 40 years ago, he led a life of ups and downs, lacking any clear direction. At one point, his excessive drinking nearly claimed his life—he coughed up massive amounts of blood. But miraculously, he recovered, embraced his faith, and became a devoted follower of Jesus. Over the next 30 years, he worked tirelessly to establish a solid track for a government-supplied electrical materials business for U.S. military bases overseas, staying in the office until 10:30 p.m. most nights. He prayed earnestly for everyone around him, pouring his energy into both his work and his faith.

He was a genuinely kind-hearted person, always sending encouraging KakaoTalk messages filled with warmth and personally driving anyone who needed a ride to San Francisco Airport despite his demanding schedule as a CEO. When he would share how precious it was to have spiritual conversations while giving rides to those in need, I felt deeply moved, seeing in him the essence of a true saint. Then, in late May, he passed away suddenly in a bicycle accident on a hill.

In the final five years of his life, Mr. Nam served at a Korean church that supported the homeless in San Francisco's Tenderloin district, offering free meals each weekend. He treated those in need with genuine compassion, never recoiling from the harsh conditions of the streets, instead reaching out with love, hugging them as friends, and welcoming them to church.

When some alumni familiar with his work would joke about his being like the saint-like Dalai Lama for his compassionate love towards the homeless, He'd laugh, saying, "How, on earth, can you guys compare me, a church elder, to the Dalai Lama?"

Last weekend, on a winter afternoon, as I returned from watching water birds and calming my spirit, my phone rang with an unfamiliar number.

I hesitated but answered, and it was his daughter, Seul-g. Recently appointed as a tenured professor in the Department of Urban Development at UC Irvine, she said, "My father's company will be closing at the end of this year, with no one to take over. While I was organizing his office, I found a scrapbook filled with your weekend essays from *Hankook Ilbo, aka The Korea Times America,* that he had carefully read and underlined. I wanted you to know that he's surely smiling down on you from above."

To have someone you can call or meet in times of loneliness is, I believe, a mark of a successful life. Visiting his office, where he always listened with kind eyes as if I were his beloved younger sibling and treated me to delicious dinners, is no longer possible. It's a painful reminder that he's no longer here, and I feel the weight of this loss deeply. This is the first time I've felt such a profound sense of deprivation since losing my parents. Why would a seemingly indifferent God allow this?

As 2020, a year filled with both sorrow and resilience, draws to a close, and the world remains engulfed in the chaos of the coronavirus, I find myself yearning to become a source of warmth for someone else. I hope to honor my senior's legacy and, in some small way, repay the debt of gratitude I feel for his life.

Chapter 7
A River Runs Through It

Biden Takes Office

2021-01-23 (Sat)

At 78 years old, Joe Biden has just been inaugurated as the 46th President of the United States, making history as the oldest person ever to assume the office. Watching on NBC, the public network that had been a source of tension for former President Trump, along with CNN, I saw a 21-gun salute fire as Biden and his party arrived at Arlington National Cemetery to lay a wreath. *Boom, boom...* Then, the limousine carrying Biden moved toward the ceremony site, lights flashing.

For the 75 million Americans who had hoped for Trump's reelection, this scene likely brings mixed emotions. Many may watch with a heavy heart or seek solace outdoors, taking walks to suppress their frustrations. Reports of 30,000 troops guarding Washington, D.C., had stirred hopes among some Trump supporters—both at home and abroad—of an unlikely twist that might pave the way for a second Trump administration. But, of course, such expectations were unrealistic. In her farewell address on Monday, First Lady Melania Trump had already suggested a peaceful transition, setting the stage for an uneventful inauguration.

At the same time, Melania Trump, dressed in a loose-fitting silk blend dress and a Gucci caftan dotted with bright, borderless orange cubes, descended the Air Force One runway at Palm Beach International Airport in Florida, waving to the crowd. Networks like CNN, critical of Trump, focused less on her farewell as first lady, emphasizing instead her low approval ratings upon departure.

Meanwhile, Biden entered the White House as the first president not welcomed by his predecessor, marking the start of a new administration in a deeply divided America. As the world's leading democracy, the United States holds a high standard: even a single-vote loss should be accepted humbly, in an election conducted with absolute fairness and objectivity. Now that Biden has taken office, many of Trump's policies are expected to be swiftly reversed by executive orders. Yet, the weight of a presidency is not like a sandcastle, easily erased—questions remain about the enduring impact of such power shifts.

While the United States advances at a deliberate pace in the name of democracy, China, America's chief challenger in global influence, races forward under the one-party efficiency of the Communist Party. Can America afford to watch this unfold passively?

As the Trump era closes, COVID-19 deaths in the United States have surpassed 400,000—a number as staggering as the crowd at the legendary Woodstock Festival in 1969 and nearly equal to American losses in World War II. This pandemic has claimed more lives than the combined toll of the five leading causes of death—stroke, Alzheimer's, diabetes, influenza, and pneumonia—an unprecedented and still-rising figure. By early May, the death toll is expected to reach 570,000, marking a crushing defeat in a pandemic originating in China and starkly revealing America's vulnerabilities.

Today, coincidentally my birthday, Biden takes office amidst this crisis and will need both restraint and wisdom to fulfill his four-year term as a unifying leader. To earn enduring respect, he must address the $6 trillion debt to China, correct the massive trade imbalance, and build an effective COVID-19 response. Crucially, he should preserve any constructive Trump policies, avoid the needless expenditure of national power, and establish a transparent, scientifically grounded election system that restores public confidence. America's fractured unity demands a leader who can rebuild trust and lay a solid democratic foundation—shouldn't these be Biden's highest priorities?

A River Runs Through It

2021-02-27 (Sat)

"Yeah! Woohoo!" I cheer, standing on the scale with my right arm raised in victory.

For dinner last night, I had some leftover Costco chicken from the day before, a vegetable sausage microwaved and roughly chopped, and a small cup of Japanese ramen—suffering these days under fierce competition from Korean ramen. I topped it all off with a shot of vodka in a soju glass and went to sleep. As I'd hoped, after avoiding carbs like rice and noodles for several days as if they were my enemy, I lost another 2 pounds overnight.

In 1946, after Korea's liberation, a young man from Japan returned to his hometown of Ulsan at the age of 25, taking on odd jobs, including managing horses. Not long after, he boarded a smuggling ship from Busan back to Shimonoseki, Japan. Although he started at the bottom in Tokyo's Shinjuku district, he never stopped reading literature in his spare time. He was captivated by the beautiful heroine in *The Sorrows of Young Werther*, the classic by German author Goethe. Exactly a year has passed since its breakout. In 1948, at 27, he founded a confectionery company called Lotte in Tokyo, named after Werther's heroine, and, along with his brothers, built it into the Lotte and Nongshim conglomerates that thrive in both Korea and Japan today. Remarkably, in 1988—the year of the Seoul Olympics—Forbes ranked him as the world's fourth richest person, a groundbreaking achievement for a Korean. He was a visionary businessman with the soul of a literary artist.

Another legendary Taiwanese figure who found success in Japan was the late Momofuku Ando (Oh Baek-bok 吳百福), who passed away in 2007. At 48, he developed the world's first instant ramen, "Chicken Ramen," founding the now-iconic NISSIN in 1958. Despite NISSIN facing fierce competition from Korean ramen companies today, Ando's tenacity is legendary. Famous for saying, "Even if I fall, I never get up empty-handed—I rise with a handful of dirt," Ando embodied the relentless determination that defines successful entrepreneurs. Their accomplishments are not random; they are built on grit, resilience, and vision.

I can't begin to describe how much more delicious the freshly grilled, piping-hot Costco chicken tastes when paired with a cold green Heineken. If I had one complaint about the Costco chicken, though, it would be that, while my fellow countrymen in North Korea would likely blame me by saying "stomach too full and spoiled" when they hear it, it's simply too much for a single person to eat in one sitting.

This morning, after showering, I stepped on the scale naked, and the digital display barely hit the magic number of 214. Then, the blue numbers flashed and dropped to 213.8 pounds. If I lose just 4 more pounds, I will have lost a total of 12 pounds in two weeks, bringing me back to my slim weight from 10 years ago.

I was as excited as I was when I first saw my name on the list of successful applicants posted on the wall at my alma mater's sports complex back in January 1978. The campus, located on the hillside behind the Dynasty's Secret Garden in Myeongnyun-dong, was where my journey began. I quickly took a picture with my newly purchased Samsung 5G phone, uploaded a post bragging about it to Facebook, and drove to the trailhead at Shoreline Lake & Park in Mountain View, right next to Google's headquarters campus.

I looked up at the mild San Francisco Bay sky, dotted with fluffy clouds, and felt a strange sense of sympathy for the residents of Texas. They were much farther south and suffering from a cold wave, while here, the weather was mild. I took my first powerful step on my morning walk, feeling energized.

The harsh winter is coming to an end, and the fields that were once drenched in rain during the rainy season are now covered in lush green grass, creating a magnificent sight. Spring has finally arrived. The gloomy winter, in which more than 500,000 people lost their lives to COVID-19, is showing signs of slowing down as spring approaches. People are getting vaccinated here and there, offering hope. No matter how difficult things may seem, the mighty river of time, carrying toy paper boats of hope, flows leisurely through all its bends and turns.

The Magnolia Falls, the Cherry Blossoms Bloom

2021-04-03 (Sat)

Waking up late on a leisurely weekend morning, I step into the bright, warm bathroom, bathed in sunlight. *Scrub, scrub...* After working the shampoo foam into my hair, I scoop a handful and apply it to my face and jawline. Carefully, I guide the razor along the rough spots that my left fingertips detect until my face is smooth. As the hot water cascades from the crown of my head down my shoulders, spine, and toes, a deep sigh escapes—a low, contented "Ah~."

Last evening, I had an important business meeting in Oakland, then swung by Dublin to meet with the client's lawyer, returning home late at night after covering around 150 miles. I sincerely hope everything goes well, as I've invested significant effort, and many people are counting on it. Yet, with any large-scale commercial real estate deal, there are always unknowns, keeping me on my toes until the end. That's the thrill and challenge of this work.

Oh my, this buyer is something else—so diligent that he'll send a text at dawn if needed. Arriving in his early twenties, he's nearly 40 years into his life in the U.S. A former infantryman, he's polished in both English and Korean. I'm often struck by the fluency of his English behind the sharp expression and glasses, while his Korean is also refined and resonant.

Back in the early 2000s, during the so-called IMF crisis, when Daewoo Group was collapsing, I worked as the branch manager for the commercial bank located inside the group's building for 3 years. That time gave me insights into the intensity with which the late Chairman Kim Woo-choong pursued global business. This buyer's resemblance to Chairman Kim—medium height and a slightly balding head—often brings back memories of the Daewoo founder's relentless drive and dedication.

Leaving Oakland, I hesitated for a moment, deciding which route to take home: the flat stretch of the 880 Freeway, crossing the bridge at the end, or the slightly winding 101 Freeway through San Francisco. Almost unconsciously, I found myself ascending the moonlit Bay Bridge. Outside my window, the ocean lay quiet and indifferent, with Alcatraz Island—famous for keeping the notorious Mafia boss Al Capone imprisoned until he was paroled for syphilis-related light dementia in 1939—floating in the bay. In the distance, where the inland waters meet the Pacific, the Golden Gate Bridge decorated the night like a scene from a postcard.

The Golden Gate Bridge's beauty is world-renowned, but each time I cross the Bay Bridge, its grandeur and elegance never fail to captivate me. I buy thick rice cakes from a Korean market there and enjoy eating them whenever I travel to Oakland, savoring a bite while gazing at the full moon rising. Inevitably, a bit of green bean paste falls on my lap as I drive, and I tell myself, "This is the last treat before I start my diet"—a familiar ritual by now. Though I've stubbornly hovered just 2 pounds above breaking my 210-pound barrier for over a month, I've managed to shed nearly 10 pounds during the pandemic. The secret? Walk rigorously and curb your appetite. When hunger pangs hit, instead of eating, I go outside for a walk to ease them. It's proven quite effective.

For a while, I envied those over 65 who could get the COVID-19 vaccine early. But as magnolia blossoms fell and cherry trees began to bloom, California's vaccine rollout opened up. Now, anyone over 50 can make an appointment, and in two weeks, it'll be available to everyone. After some clicking and scrolling, I finally secured my first dose in about 20 days. I feel sorry for my friends in Korea who are still struggling to access the vaccine, but I see the light at the end of this long tunnel—the sense that the biggest ordeal of my life is beginning to end.

I dream of going to Times Square for a victory celebration, the end of this "World War III against COVID-19." I want to share a jubilant kiss like the sailor in that iconic photo, surrounded by loved ones who've endured this long period of hardship and resilience. Let's go.

Cauliflower Love in May

2021-05-08 (Sat)

Tok. Tok. Click. Click. All set. Wow! It didn't even take 20 seconds.

I had just changed my oil a month ago with only 1,200 miles since, but my dashboard kept flashing the "check engine oil and filter" message. So, I drove over to the oil change shop and asked them to take a look. The owner, a friendly guy, had me step out for a moment, then hopped into the driver's seat. With a few quick taps on the reset menu, the pesky error message vanished. "Awesome!" I thanked him with a fist bump. It's always a pleasure to receive top-notch service from someone who knows their stuff. Running an oil shop is no easy business, with so many car models and resets to manage.

With my mood lifted by the excellent service, I headed for a walk along the beach, humming along to *Summer Wine*—the 1967 hit by Nancy Sinatra and Lee Hazelwood. Sinatra, Frank's daughter, was 27 at the time, and now, in her 80s, that duet still resonates. On the way back, I stopped at Costco to pick up some eggs. Near the entrance, a vibrant display of red roses greeted me, nudging out other seasonal products, a reminder that Mother's Day is here once again.

May truly is the month of family and love. On May 5th, Children's Day, I remember how we'd line up in the elementary school playground to receive a small gift—a 20-won Samlip Cream Sandwich. It was a simple treat, two halves of soft bread with a thin layer of white cream, but it felt as special as a birthday. We'd think of Sopa Bang Jeong-hwan, the pioneer who established Children's Day, and silently thank him. Three days later, it was Mother's Day, and we'd buy carnations from the stationery store, carefully pinning them onto our mothers' and grandmothers' chests with clothespins as a small token of our love.

"Forgetting all the pain of giving birth, Trying day and night to grow me well."

This is a Mother's Day song lyric praising Mom's unconditional love toward us. Literally, it meant mom would not bother remembering how painful she was giving birth to us.

On Mother's Day during elementary school, Yoon-young—one of the girl's boys admired. When she went out to the podium to play the piano, the rest of us would sing together along to her piano playing. Playing the piano was only a dream for us boys in the hillside poor neighbor. When she reached this part of the song, my throat would tighten, and with reddened eyes, I'd glance up at the ceiling, pausing at the moment. Even now, more than ten years since my mother passed away and with my 60th birthday behind me, it still affects me just the same.

"Come on! The vendor brought in some nice, large potatoes for mashed potatoes—they're as big as Daehongdan(N. Korean Heights famous for producing big potatoes) potatoes. I'll set a few aside for you. They're delicious." This heartwarming call was from H, who is my senior by 7 years in college and the youngest son of a displaced family from Hamgyeong Province, N. Korea, during the Korean War. After graduating, he started his career as a bachelor physics teacher at Pyeongtaek High School, right next to Osan Air Base, where I began my service as a second lieutenant in 1983. During his two years there, his family immigrated to the United States at the invitation of his eldest sister, a Seoul National University nursing graduate who'd secured a job in the U.S. Arriving in America, he and his older brother, a Seoul National University graduate as well, enrolled at UC Davis with big dreams. But H. eventually left his studies, helping his brother complete his doctorate more easily and working part-time jobs at Home Depot and elsewhere to support his family.

At 42, he and his wife took over an American steakhouse in Sunnyvale, which they ran successfully for 27 years, becoming well-known restaurateurs and eventually purchasing a large home in one of Silicon Valley's wealthiest neighborhoods. Now, as Silicon Valley's redevelopment craze transforms the area, nearly all the 20 stores in his shopping center have been pushed out, leaving just three. Fortunately, H. has some time left on his lease and is negotiating a buyout with the new owner. If an agreement is reached, he's planning to retire without regrets. Laughing, he tells me about his restaurant journey and his hands-on approach—fixing equipment and handling every detail.

"If I'm born again, I'll never work in a restaurant," he jokes. "I'm so tired of it. Did you finish the cauliflower I gave you? I'll give you more."

This time of fresh green, the blue of May, is a beautiful season for us—a season full of love and gratitude.

"No worries, Everyone Makes Mistake"

2021-06-12 (Sat)

"Duckhwan, you already know more than 90% of people in this world. You don't need to understand the complex formulas that only actuaries and math majors grasp."

This was Dave's response when I, the type who prefers to be fully prepared before teaching others or taking on responsibilities, asked him a detailed question. His advice was a reminder that just as you'll never learn to swim if you wait until you know everything perfectly, chasing excessive perfection can waste precious time.

The powerful voice on the other end of the Zoom screen belongs to my 70-year-old mentor, Dave, who spent 20 years as the general manager at the San Jose regional headquarters before retiring and shifting to educational consulting for Farmer's agency owners. Occasionally, he gets frustrated when I ask questions he feels I should know by now, but he's a good-natured person at heart.

Today's training session, following lessons on business, Work-Comp, and home insurance, focused on life insurance. Despite completing the intensive five-week program at Farmers University, learning truly never ends. We delved into *Universal Life*, which, due to its flexibility, now holds nearly 70% of the permanent life insurance market, even though it's costlier than *Term Life*, a simpler, fixed-term product without cash value.

As the nearly hour-long, one-on-one Zoom training wrapped up, a smile spread across my face. I felt a deep sense of pride—not just for immigrating at 42 or for making a life in the U.S. over these past 20 years, but for becoming an agency owner in a field I now consider my specialty. To sit through an hour of Zoom training with an American consultant, discussing complex products and asking in-depth questions in English—it felt like a true accomplishment.

I was immature to think, even for a moment, that merely understanding the content of my work would automatically translate to earning money. Reality doesn't work that way. It's only when I go beyond the self-satisfaction of understanding and actually sell the service to someone that it becomes meaningful.

Unless I'm running a renowned cold noodle restaurant where diners flock in groups, willing to wait in long lines for the chef's legendary flavors, no one is going to come to me voluntarily to buy my product or service. Whether it's asking acquaintances or advertising through newspapers and the Internet, selling is the foundation of all economic activity. Yet, there's a long-standing cultural stigma in Korean history that ranks commerce and industry below other pursuits, leading to a kind of inherited hesitation around selling.

Even when approaching people I know, I often find myself coughing awkwardly to begin, sometimes breaking into a cold sweat or feeling my face flush at the thought of rejection. But the way to overcome this psychological barrier is to recognize that nearly everyone in the world lives by selling something. To succeed, you must develop resilience, realizing that rejection is not personal. If someone declines, there's no need for embarrassment—just wipe away the heavy feelings with a virtual eraser and move on to the next person. *Eruhwa*, as they say—no worries, everyone makes mistakes!

With 15 years of experience in real estate brokerage, I've reached a point where I can manage my time by focusing on the big picture. However, given the highs and lows tied to economic cycles and market conditions, I often found myself daydreaming. Recently, I've been busy channeling that experience into the insurance field. Although I passed my insurance license exam about 10 years ago, it mostly stayed in the background, costing me a $500 renewal fee every two years. Now, I'm finally putting it to use, learning from skilled professionals in areas that were once unfamiliar to me—Business, Work-Comp, auto, home, and life insurance.

This journey has truly humbled me, making me realize how vast the world is and how much there still is to learn. I've come to see that everything, in a way, is connected to real estate, and insurance touches nearly every corner of life. For newcomers to the U.S. who are unsure of their career path, I'd wholeheartedly recommend diving into the insurance or finance field without hesitation. Even if your English feels limited, don't let that hold you back. Starting now, little by little, your English will improve, revealing its potential along the way.

The Hydrangeas In Lombard Street

2021-07-17 (Sat)

Daffodil? No... What was the name of this flower, so delicate in color and blooming so beautifully?

It's already been two years since the spring of 2019, the year before the pandemic. Thinking back, it reminds me of a time from 50 years ago when I was in elementary school. Chaesik, the top student among the girls and an impressive speaker, was admired by all of us boys navigating our way through adolescence. Recently, after reconnecting on a BAND, an online alumni SNS, she visited the U.S. for the first time, and we met again—nearly 50 years later.

After dropping off her luggage at her uncle's place in Garden Grove, where he now lives as a respected grandfather, Chaesik rented a car with her sister—two years my senior and also an accomplished former honors student—and they drove up to San Francisco, where I live. It was early April, a bit too soon for the flowers to fully bloom, so we admired what we could—like the charming, winding path of Lombard Street. But this past Sunday, returning to Lombard Street, I was met by a stunning sight: vibrant hydrangeas in full bloom, brightening the scene. With fewer tourists than before the pandemic, the quiet beauty felt even more special. Wanting to share, I filmed a video while driving slowly down the street and posted it in our alumni group. It almost felt as though I could hear my old friends' enthusiastic reactions.

Since completing my vaccinations in early June, I've finally felt comfortable enough to venture out. But for the past two years, even short drives felt like a chore, and I rarely left town. Not too long ago, I would take weekend drives to Santa Cruz, stroll along the Boardwalk, enjoy lunch at a lavender-scented café, and then head up Highway 1 to the Pigeon Point Lighthouse to catch the sunset over the stunning Pescadero coastline.

Sitting on a quiet bench by the lighthouse, gazing out over the vast Pacific, I'm filled with memories of the streets of my hometown, which were full of people. Sentimentality takes hold, and I find myself muttering, *"I'm growing old in this foreign land."*

The sunset on the deserted coast, shaped by the evening sun dipping past Honolulu, Hawaii, was so mesmerizing that I was lost in thought until the darkness quietly enveloped everything around me. From there, I drove north along the scenic Pacific Coast Highway 1, which led me to Half Moon Bay, a stretch as stunning as Monterey but with fewer cars. I turned right onto Highway 92, crossing the lush mountains leading to Crystal Springs Reservoir and then onto the famous 280 Freeway, once hailed as the world's most beautiful highway. Heading south about 30 miles, I returned home, completing a perfect 150-mile Sunday drive.

Last Sunday, I decided to go further, pushing myself out of the usual pandemic radius. Initially, I planned to spend the day near Half Moon Bay, walking along unnamed cliffs where wildflowers were blooming, but I ended up in San Francisco, where the vibrant streets offered a refreshing change.

There, I stopped to greet Mr. P, an 80-year-old who has run a liquor store near the famous Lombard Street for nearly 30 years. Spending the day exploring the road and Fisherman's Wharf was a welcome escape from pandemic thoughts. My connection with Mr. P is a treasure—he's been a dedicated *Hankook Ilbo, aka The Korea Times America, aka The Korea Times America* reader, for decades. About five years ago, after reading one of my essays, he reached out to connect, and since then, we've shared stories bridging generations. Relationships like this, formed through shared reflections and mutual respect, feel rare and beautiful.

When I think of this man's tenacity—immigrating to an unfamiliar country like the United States and protecting his livelihood for decades—I feel a deep sense of respect. Few people have reached out to me in such heartfelt ways, like the rare calls from LA or the comments shared over a round of golf, reminding me of how precious and invaluable these relationships are. Could I have ever imagined that such beautiful connections would come into my life?

Even as the mutated pandemic rises after the vaccine, life remains a journey where, ultimately, each of us must return to the heavens after our time in this beautiful world. If we can weave heart patterns from these threads of dharma, nurturing them day by day, what more could we wish for in this life?

I Miss you, Auntie

2021-09-11 (Sat)

"Oh, you're asking me again and again, even though I already replied I am from Gwangju, Jeoolado?"

My lifelong rival, now best friend—my sister, who's three years older and lives in Yangsan, Gyeongnam—teased me in our first KakaoTalk chat in a while. We giggled behind our screens, reconnecting after some time. A few months back, I'd noticed a KakaoTalk photo of her looking noticeably thinner, which worried me. I sent her a few hundred dollars and urged her to get a checkup. Thankfully, the early signs of throat cancer were caught, and with chemotherapy, she managed to prevent it from advancing.

The Honam dialect she was playfully imitating is one I remember fondly from childhood. My friend Jongmo's mom, whom I met back in 1964, spoke it. We use to call her Aunty. That was around the time my parents, who had faced business setbacks, moved us from a mansion in Dongdaesin-dong, Seo-gu, Busan to a rented room on a hill in Cheongpa-dong, Yongsan-gu. For a few months, our view overlooked the trains at Seoul Station. In 1965, just before I started elementary school, we settled into a thatched-roof house on a cliff in Donam-dong, Seongbuk-gu, Seoul.

When we finally had to leave Donam-dong due to

redevelopment, our families relocated together, moving from Jangwi-dong to Suyu-ri and then Ui-dong, Seoul. Both fathers passed before turning 50 or 60, but the bond between our mothers remained strong. I'd drop by their home without a second thought, whether my friends were there or not like it was my own. On each visit, my friend's mother would prepare a delicious meal, whether it was lunch or dinner.

Though we grew up bickering and competing over who was right, once we were both married with young children, we shared countless outings together, forming deep family bonds. Every season, we'd visit places like Ui-dong Green Park and Doseonsa Temple or enjoy the azaleas in spring and the maple leaves in fall. We aimed to pass our friendship to the next generation, ensuring our children became lifelong friends. We were more than close friends and neighbors; we were inseparable.

In January 1975, after completing the joint high school entrance exam, Jongmo and I—both navigating adolescence—set off on our first adventure. We traveled on the Honam Line to visit her maternal uncle's home in Hak-dong, Gwangju-si, Jeollanam-do. Her uncle, Cho Byeong-cheol, was the Dean of Student Affairs at Chosun University. We would lie with our chins resting on our palms, lying on the warm floor, enjoying roasted Garaetteok (sausage-sized *and shaped white Korean rice cake)* dipped in soy sauce, prepared by his high school-aged older cousin. Songs like Lee Jang-hee's "I'll Give You Everything" drifted from the transistor, sparking endless daydreams about our future partners and where they might be

Three days later, we visited Hwasun, which would become the base of the Gwangju Democratization Movement just a few years later. We took a winding intercity bus ride through Jeolla-do's mountain roads, arriving in Boknae-myeon, Boseong-gun. After changing buses, passing through Beolgyo—famous for dried pollack—we finally reached her grandfather's house late at night in Yuleo-myeon, Boseong-gun, a place renowned for its green tea. Jongmo's grandfather, Mr. Je, Dal-dong, a Confucian scholar, welcomed us, and over the next few days, I watched rustic rice cakes being made on a straw stove and even joined in a friendly soccer match with local kids. Showing off a flashy feint I'd learned in the city, and I drew excited reactions from my new countryside friends.

From there, we traveled to *his* maternal grandparents' home in Jangpyeong-up (Now very famous as the birthplace of the 2024 Nobel Literature Laureate, Han Gang), Jangheung-gun, where the Yeongsan River Estuary Development Project had just begun. The house, with its whale-backed tile roof, reflected our family's heritage. I was taken aback when I tried Jeolla-do-style New Year's rice cake soup, served with a whole chicken head—a vivid memory that feels like yesterday.

In the early '70s, even in our mountain village, where life was tough and everyone was poor, Jongmo's family always seemed to stand out. His father worked as a librarian at the National Library of Korea and was renowned as a bibliographer, so their home was filled with hundreds of old books, some centuries old, which he would sometimes sell or donate. Aunty, meanwhile, spent her days at a side job, frugally sewing dozens of first patterns of suits alongside her friends, who were moms of our elementary school female juniors who had funny nicknames like Injeong-ine, Bejjang-ine and Yongja-ne.

Their hard work paid off—they were the first family in the neighborhood to own modern plumbing, an iron cabinet, a gramophone that played Neil Sedaka's *You Mean Everything to Me*, and even a television.

When I was in middle school, my sister, only three years older than me, and I got into a fight over something trivial. She threw a few of my neatly plastic-wrapped textbooks into the yard, leaving me feeling deeply wounded. The argument quickly escalated into a full-blown shouting match, drawing attention from the entire neighborhood. Each time, the kind Aunty from the house below would come running up with a concerned look, breaking up the fight with a gentle shout, "Hey, stop it now."

My mother, who worked tirelessly as a salesperson at an insurance company, would come home each evening, clearly worn out. She would often listen to Auntie's reporting of the fight, saying, "Hyungnim (Big sister), Eunyoung, that b*tch," and she would usually tell my mother about my older sister's mischievous activities—My mom was 12 years older than the Auntie—and take my side, offering me a moment of comfort and understanding. Today, as I walked through the parking lot on my way to work, I saw a single paulownia leaf drifting across the pavement—a subtle reminder that autumn had arrived. Regret washed over me for not visiting the kind Aunty more often while she was alive, a mother who had been so kind to us and who left this world over ten years ago.

"Are you watching over us from heaven, Aunty? Until we meet again... goodbye."

The Flower of Blessings

2021-10-02 (Sat)

"Usually, the mother says she will raise the child?"

These words came from my friend Dissally—a petite, gentle Ethiopian man in his second marriage whom I hadn't seen since the pandemic began in April of last year. I can say, without hesitation, that reconnecting with him has been truly delightful. We've known each other for nearly a decade. We used to meet at the Jacuzzi at the nearby YMCA.

One of my quirks is a struggle with remembering names, especially foreign ones. Even when someone gives me their full name, I tend to focus on their expressions and faces, often finding myself embarrassed later, wondering if they were "Robert" or "Andrew." This time, determined not to forget, I pinched the flesh by my belly button as a reminder and promptly saved his name in my smartphone contacts.

Ethiopia has a special place in my mind. It's one of the 16 UN member states that sent troops to support South Korea during the Korean War. The memorable names of Emperor Haile Selassie, the capital city Addis Ababa, and Bikila Abebe—who ran barefoot and became as celebrated as soccer legend Pele half a century ago—all come to mind. Ethiopia stands unique as the only African country to fiercely resist European (Italian) colonial invasion, maintaining a strong sense of national pride. Dissally once mentioned that he is of mixed race, with his mother hailing from Eritrea, which gained independence from Ethiopia in 1993. His father died in combat with the Eritrean Liberation Front 40 years ago when Dissally was just a child. In his gentle demeanor, I now understand the hint of loneliness in his expression.

The pandemic has certainly changed lifestyles in many ways. Few people are returning to the YMCA, which now operates at reduced hours, and many longtime members of 10 or 20 years have shifted to other fitness centers offering longer hours. It's easy to guess that the YMCA's existence is facing challenges. My friend Dissally, now working full-time as a cook at Facebook's cafeteria in Menlo Park, mentioned he'd already prepaid a year's membership at his new gym and, with the added convenience, doesn't see a reason to return to the YMCA.

Our conversation soon turned to his 23-year-old son, Heyab, who looked just like him but a bit taller. Heyab, the youngest participant in the YMCA's Saturday *Deep Water Aqua Boot Camp*, was always a favorite among the mostly 60-plus-year-old class, bringing youthful energy to the pool. Heyab majored in Business at Foothill Community College in Los Altos Hills and then transferred to San Jose State University, graduated during the pandemic, found a good job, and has since become independent. Dissally sighed with relief, feeling this was a reward for the years he spent as a single father. His son chose to live with him after his divorce, and Dissally raised him alone for 15 years before, finally, the weight lifted as Heyab made his way in the world.

Just before the pandemic, Dissally remarried—a 34-year-old Ethiopian woman, 18 years his junior, as beautiful as the calla lily, Ethiopia's national flower. She cares for him deeply and loves him as if he were her own, and Dissally now says he's on cloud nine, living with immense happiness. I wholeheartedly congratulated him, adding that, in Korean culture, you are to be called a Dodong-num (thief) by taking such a young wife, which made him laugh. I admitted that while a young partner has its appeal, I'd probably avoid a large age gap, joking that I might become so infatuated I'd wear myself out like a radish dried in the sun. Dissally laughed, saying my worries were unfounded—it's just daily happiness, he assured me.

"Wow, it really is that good," I mused, and he nodded with a smile as if savoring every word.

What is love? It's not complicated. It's 'sex with genuine interest and affection.' Recently, the vile and absurd insults that a leading presidential candidate from the ruling party hurled at the wife of his older brother have become the talk of the town. The mystery of the female body, something that should remain delicately veiled in the subconscious, has now been pulled out into the open, leaving me with a bitter sense of self-reflection about the absurd state of things. But anyway. Would I shy away from a much younger woman even if she approached me, like the captivating Diachan, who is one of the four Gyeongguk Gyeongseong (Chinese great beauties) favored by Dong Zhuo in Romance of the Three Kingdoms? I think I would. (p.s. The Four Great Beauties are four Chinese women who were renowned for their beauty. They are usually identified as Xi Shi, Wang Zhaojun, Diaochan, and Yang Yuhuan).

The day before yesterday, after helping a client find a small retail shop in Santa Clara's Koreatown, I treated myself to an early dinner with soondae (Korean sausage) soup at a place called 'Obok' (It means five blessings) in the same mall. The taste brought back the familiar comfort of my hometown, soothing my longing for the flavors of home I'd left behind. When we talk about the five blessings, aren't they longevity, wealth, health, children, and even teeth? It's easy to agree that the blessing of companionship, especially for a man, is an essential one, inseparable from any other blessing in life.

Love in Silicon Valley

2021-11-06 (Sat)

Ding-dong, the mobile text message bell chimed, and a message appeared on the screen. "How are you feeling?" This was the text message from H, sent just before He boarded a United flight from SFO to Denver to visit his future in-laws. As I read my senior's message expressing concern over my appearance the previous night, the chill in my heart warmed under the morning autumn sunlight.

H and his future in-laws first connected at UC Davis in 1977 when we were both studying abroad. He dropped out to start a business and eventually moved to San Jose, as did another family—my future in-laws—who relocated after finishing their doctorates. These two families were first-generation immigrant neighbors who, years before, had raised their children together.

Later, H's in-law's family took over a large wine shop and moved to Colorado about 20 years ago, and the families lost touch. Then, as if by fate, my future father-in-law, on a business trip to San Jose, happened to stop by the steakhouse H used to own. Who would have thought that, after 20 years, a simple visit would reconnect these families, transforming them from old neighbors to future in-laws?

The prospective son-in-law of H, who was 3 years older than his daughter, had grown up with her in elementary and middle school. He had been helping her father run their wine business, but even into his forties, he had yet to marry, which concerned his parents. With an eye on H's two lovely daughters, the parents started to wonder how both families might once again grow close in a new way.

While the clever, quick-witted younger daughter found her match early, securing a lovely single-family home in Silicon Valley with her parents' help and settling into the bliss of newlywed life, her father can't help but feel mixed emotions about her older sister. Now in her late thirties, the older daughter has been living alone and working in New York for years. The senior feels both guilt and pity, reflecting on how he raised her with a strict, almost military-style discipline during her teenage years—leftover methods from his days in the As he lives his life now, he says he can't help but sigh, reflect, and even beat his chest in regret.

Hearing him talk so animatedly about orchestrating a "ninth-inning comeback" marriage for his eldest daughter, I couldn't help but get excited, too. It made me long to visit Colorado one day—it must be as beautiful as people say. I want to see Lowry AFB in Denver, where the U.S. Air Force Training Command is located and where my close friend, Captain Bruce, was stationed. Bruce, who had served in the Tactical Intelligence Group at Osan Air Base on a one-year TDY (Temporary Duty) and as a new second lieutenant assigned to the ROKAF Combat Air Command, might still be there. And, of course, I want to see Colorado Springs, home of the U.S. Air Force Academy.

I think of John Denver, who named himself after the city,

drawn by Colorado's beauty, immortalizing it in country folk songs like "Annie's Song." I've searched for Captain Bruce on Facebook, but there's no trace. Perhaps, like my senior's soon-to-be in-law, if I visit the base in person, finding him might be as easy as asking around.

I shared this story with a senior member of my college alumni association in the San Francisco Bay Area—a longtime supporter of mine—who gave me a fair amount of flak, saying, "Didn't you know that?" (Ugh). This was back in the summer of 1987, when I was a rookie banker in a company after my military service, trying my best to be recognized and eventually get posted to a U.S. branch. I was studying my banking field work manual when I crossed paths with Captain Bruce, who had come back to Korea for two weeks to participate in the Team Spirit joint military exercise in Seoul.

The only church experience I'd had was from a childhood visit to the Donam-dong Evangelism Center with a friend in fifth grade when I was around twelve. They'd promised boiled eggs to visitors, and the entire church would be packed, with a big drum beating and people chanting, "I can hear the voice of angels~." Church customs and settings were foreign to me, so when Bruce asked me to show him the largest church in the world, I had no idea what he meant. It was completely absurd that I didn't know about the Yoido Full Gospel Church, founded by the late famous Korean Pastor David Yonggi Cho, who had just passed away two months ago. I wanted to explain that perhaps it was due to limited newspaper coverage, but I knew that excuse wouldn't hold up.

After a while, Senior L, who had celebrated his 70th birthday just the day before with a small dinner gathering, called as well. He was feeling quite worried about me—he was 6-year junior and a chair of the alumni association. It had been ten years since Senior L lost his wife to breast cancer. She had been his steadfast support, working as the head nurse at Ewha Mokdong Hospital when he was working as the Korean branch manager for a leading American mainframe company. Since her passing, he had been living a solitary life, like a lonely bird separated from its flock. His son worked in Korea, and his daughter in New Jersey, so they could only send a bouquet of flowers to mark his 70th birthday. Celebrating without family at a table that should have been filled with joy, I couldn't ignore the cold sweat trickling down my back or the feverish warmth rising within me.

The intensity of the past few days had worn me down. I'd been singularly focused as a major deal neared its final stages, and with the back-to-back toasts during Senior L's 70th birthday celebration, I was truly feeling it. To make things worse, my 90% polyester dress shirt, which thankfully resisted wrinkles, lacked any breathability, and I was generating so much heat that I felt like I was going to pass out. Eventually, I couldn't take it anymore—I stepped outside, took off the shirt, and let the cool air bring me back to life. Somehow, I made it home, emptied my system, took a long, hot shower, and drifted off into a deep, much-needed sleep.

This morning, I'm back at my desk, typing as if yesterday's exhaustion was just a dream. The love and care of my seniors truly worked magic, reminding me once again that the best remedy of all is love.

3355 Torrance

2021-12-11 (Sat)

Oversleeping got me to the gym a full 40 minutes late, which meant missing out on swimming today. Still, there's no way I'd skip the hot tub and steam room—absolutely essential. My weight has been creeping up, not drastically, but enough to make me take notice. It's probably not from comfort or laziness but my rekindled love affair with Korean food lately. Spicy ramen, CJ brand steamed vegetables on top of rice hotpots, Ttokbokki, rice cakes—you name it. I've been indulging in all kinds of carb-loaded treats throughout the Thanksgiving holiday, and it's starting to show.

There's a fascinating irony in the story of the Samsung Group, which remains a powerhouse in Korea. The Late Chairman Lee Byung-Chul of the SAMSUNG Group gave the group as an inheritance to his third son, Lee Kun-hee, while a smaller portion was given to the first son, Lee Maeng-hee. The smaller portion is currently known as CJ Food and Entertainment Group.

As I glance back with only a couple of weeks left in the year, my wallet's still comfortably full... If I could wrap up the year without major worries, I'd be thrilled, I'd catch up with friends and would hum along to the very lively Korean old folk song of 'Miryang Aririang', of which lyrics goes like "Dear love, please look at me excitedly like you've seen the rare flower in the deep winter.". But here I am, feeling inexplicably low. Is it just a passing whim, or maybe a lack of gratitude creeping in?

"Oh, it's hot…" I say as I slap some alcohol-based aftershave on my face in the powder room and catch my reflection. The nearly 100-kilo figure staring back has me pondering the durability of my Korean hair dye. It covers in 7-8 minutes, sure, but judging by the way Gray sneaks back in, it doesn't exactly last. I see myself decked out in a snug, white, short-sleeved spandex workout top, the result of rigorous sets of K-squats and push-ups. My upper body looks taut, almost ready to burst, with two small nipples dotting my chest, a reminder of the muscle I've earned through the grind.

A Christmas carol should be ringing out on the bustling streets of department stores, filling the air with a festive spirit. But what is this? The year-end atmosphere feels completely hollow this time, dimmed by the news that many countries are closing their borders again due to the spread of the new COVID-19 variant, 'Omicron'—a Greek letter no one had really heard of until now.

This surge has forced me to postpone my plans to bring my two older sisters from Korea to California and Las Vegas. Every year, I look forward to hosting my beloved siblings and relatives, sharing in the warmth and joy of family, but life, it seems, always finds a way to complicate the simplest of plans. It's a special thing to be grateful for the family we're born into, those who share our joys and struggles, or the friends we make along the way who bring meaning and support into our lives.

Reflecting on this, I remember that when I first announced my plan to start a new business, the earliest clients to contact me were my loyal readers from the *Hanguk Ilbo, aka The Korea Times America*, who sent encouraging messages on KakaoTalk and shared personal stories of their own. When I counted, there were more than just a few. Truly, life brings us many cherished connections in unexpected ways.

Last Thanksgiving, I made an impromptu drive to LA—the first time I'd headed down there in over a year. The roads were packed with holiday traffic, with even the side routes and back roads jammed. It took at least three hours to cross the 104-mile Pacheco Pass Caifornia Hwy 152, the stretch that links Gilroy to Interstate 5. Instead of feeling impatient, though, I felt a spark of excitement. LA was my first home in the U.S., where I'd spent my first two months after arriving from Korea in January 2002.

The day after I arrived, I had the good fortune to meet an acquaintance for lunch, which I had only loosely planned. What I hadn't expected was the chance to meet my future daughter-in-law for the very first time—and to have dinner with my son. She, born in the U.S. to a Korean family, spoke flawless Korean, bridging our worlds seamlessly. Although she doesn't know much about old idioms or proverbs, like old story about how Chinese young horse keeper from the countryside could save his life from a war when he broke his leg falling from a horse and dodge the draft.

They'd met through a dating app, fell in love, and a month ago, they moved in together in a new apartment in Koreatown. The joy of seeing them happy lifted me immensely. When I think of the countless lonely people still searching for companionship, I can't help but feel deeply grateful for this moment. Their apartment, completed in 2019, had all the comforts and elegance of a modern hotel—a fitting beginning for them. Watching them, I felt at ease, knowing that they were on a good path, and I left with the happy thought that a house and marriage may well be on the horizon for the next year.

Both of them are CPAs, and both work at stable companies, so a bright future together feels assured. I couldn't just drop everything and call my friends during Thanksgiving weekend to hang out—everyone had their family plans. After all, life isn't something we can just organize on a whim. Instead, I took a two-day solo hike to Griffith Park and a small suburb hill where I could watch Mount Baldy, Southern California's highest peak, taking the chance to reset and improve my health. This rare trip south brought some peace of mind, and after returning quietly to San Francisco, I felt refreshed.

This time, though, I made it a point to reach out to a couple of close comrades from the 78th R.O.K Air Force Cadet Class. We arranged to meet at a Korean pub called "Samsamohoh,",meaning 3355 in street number which the restaurant was also named after in Torrance. One whom I met 20 years ago in LA, and the other is for the first time in 35 years since my discharge from the ROK Air Force. As we sat there, it felt as though time had raced past, its marks visible in thinning hairlines and deepening lines on our faces.

To all of you who have stayed resilient through this tumultuous year, I offer my warm regards as we approach year's end. With this final essay of the year, on its last weekend, I wish you peace and strength for the days to come.

Chapter 8
Half Moon Bay's Dobermann

Miss You Aunt

2022-01-22 (sat)

"Aunt in Daeshin-dong, Busan, had stomach cancer some time ago and had some part of her stomach removed. Now, she can barely tolerate even a simple seaweed soup. My other Aunty in Goejeong, who attends the daycare center at Beomeosa Temple, isn't doing well either. They're both ninety now." With that in mind, I sent them some money.

I rarely saw my Aunties growing up, but whenever I did, they welcomed me with the warmest, most affectionate smiles. It's been decades since I last visited them in person. Even when I lived in Korea, I'd only hear about them in passing, snippets of family news like leaves carried by the wind. And after immigrating to the U.S. twenty years ago, my short trips back rarely allowed time to visit everyone properly.

Thankfully, my youngest aunt, who isn't yet in her eighties, and my uncle, a former baseball player from Gyeongnam Commercial High School, are both doing well. My uncle, especially, is still going strong in his early eighties, and I'm sure she's less lonely than the two aunts. With the New Year, old memories of my aunts from childhood surfaced, and so, I sent my sister 500,000 won, telling her to treat them to a nice meal.

She shared this story with me on KakaoTalk messanger, bringing back those cherished memories.

I vividly remember my aunt in Daeshin-dong, the third in our family. She always showed deep respect for my mom because mom was the first lady of the family and six years older than her. She called my mom "hyung-nim," hyung-nim meaning big sister, with warmth and admiration. My mind drifts back 48 years to the winter of 1975, right before I was set to start high school. It was a freezing January day in Korea, and the fierce cold, as relentless as today, seemed to chill everything it touched.

The eldest son of my Aunt was named Su-hwan who was three years senior to me. He was a rookie private first class at an Army Division led by a famous division commander who was a front runner of the 8th class of the Korea Military Academy on the Western Front, and it was on that day we all went to visit cousin army soldier who was a private first class on base. He was stationed there under Division Commander Kim Bok-dong, who was well-known not just for his role but as the elder brother of Kim Ok-sook, who went on to become the First Lady beside the late President Roh Tae-woo.

Along with cousins of my age, we took the Tongilho Express from Busan, armed with rice cakes and an assortment of other delicacies. After spending the night at my house in Donam-dong, we set off again, heading to Bulkwang-dong Intercity Bus Terminal the following morning to catch the bus for the next leg of the journey. Today, with Jayuro (Freedom HWY) open, you can reach Munsan Imjingak from Seoul in about an hour. But back then, Subway Line 1 had only recently begun operations, and it took us a solid hour just to get from

Donam-dong to the Bulkwang-dong terminal.

After finally reaching Munsan, we transferred to an intercity bus that took us through a series of stops—Yeoncheon, Jeongok, Geumchon, Paju, and Bongilcheon. It felt like it took three or four hours altogether, each transfer adding another layer to the journey's memory.

As the aunt carefully unpacked her bundle, out came a treasure trove of homemade delights—sirutteok, yakgwa, japchae, tangerines, boiled eggs, and a whole fried chicken that had traveled on the Gyeongbu (Seoul-Busan) Line train, still warm even after a day on the journey. She laid everything on the small one person floor seat dining table in the visiting room set up in the corner of the PX building near the guard post. Private First Class Kim Su-hwan, with his sun-tanned face and hunched shoulders from six months in the unit, broke into a broad smile. He eagerly dug into the sirutteok, gulping down Chilseong Cider to wash it all down, savoring every bite of this special home-cooked meal after such a long time. Watching him enjoy it so much made the experience all the more joyful.

My "beloved aunt," a lively beauty in her early 40s and a former cheerleader from N Girls' High School, one of Busan's top schools, looked on at her eldest son with a mixture of pride and sadness. She hadn't seen him in six months. My soldier cousin had grown up with all the privileges, thanks to his dad, my uncle, a legal reporter for *Kukje Shinbo*, a prominent daily in Busan. He was the pride of our family, so we cousins had heard endless tales about him, especially during the year he stayed with us in Donam-dong to prepare for his college entrance exams, attending an academy in Jongno. Yet, one day, without much notice, he surprised us all by enlisting.

Seated at a table beside the fireplace, bustling with

visitors and warmed by rising steam from a pitcher of barley tea, my little Aunty looked at my soldier cousin with a concerned expression and asked, "Isn't it hard for you?" Private Fist Clast Kim, whose skin was tanned dark as a farmhand's from countless hours under the unforgiving winter sun, leaned in and began to spin tales of his military life, each story slightly embellished to impress. As he recounted one particular tale of a bully he suffered from his senior soldiers and barracks camaraderie, I felt a chill down my spine, thinking, "What, in just 3 or 4 years, that'll be me?"

The story he shared has stayed vivid all these years. It went like this: During a routine inspection, the veteran soldiers were relentless with the recruits, demanding impeccable cleanliness. When they found evidence of someone having "taken care of urgent business" around the barracks, they commanded, "Confess while I'm asking nicely." When no one stepped forward out of sheer terror, the veterans dug up the offending material with a field shovel, stirred it into a drum of water, and ordered each soldier to drink a bowlful. And they did. It was beyond belief. Thankfully, my own service passed without ever witnessing such an absurd spectacle of military hazing, and I'm forever grateful to the heavens for that mercy.

Dear aunts, this is me now, sending my heartfelt wishes to you. With the Lunar New Year fast approaching, I hope you are blessed with long lives and good health. Happy New Year of the Im-In, Tiger!

Edelweiss in San Francisco

2022-02-26 (sat)

'Pirik pirik, hiyo, hoho, hoio. Chirp chir...' Oh my gosh... How could the world be this beautiful? Late at night, on my way home from work, I paused outside my front gate. In the branches of a lush, unknown tree, a bird called out persistently. Even when I flashed my camera toward the branches, it continued to sing, invisible but insistent, for over ten minutes, making no move to show itself or fly away. Was it a canary, or perhaps a cuckoo? Its call was as lovely as 'jade beads rolling on a silver platter,' a sound I've longed to hear at least once in my life. For a moment, I lost myself in the comforting fantasy that it might be my mother, who passed away ten years ago, coming to congratulate me.

Reflecting on the publishing company in Seoul that worked so passionately to bring my book to life, I can't help but feel grateful. They crafted the banner and event pamphlet (for congratulation ceremony) with an impressive professionalism and dedication. Korea's publishing capabilities, if summed up in one phrase, would simply be "Awesome." Their skill is on par with Korea's globally recognized advancements in industries like semiconductors, automobiles, shipbuilding, and, of course, K-pop. Watching their meticulous attention to detail in each Kakao Talk message and email reminds me of the spirit that defines Koreans: 'If you can do it, do it; if not, make it happen.' It's a relentless drive that I'd almost forgotten in my two decades of living in the U.S.

It still doesn't feel real—that the title "writer" is now attached to my name. Looking back, I realize how much my younger brother, five years my junior and once a student of creative writing, influenced me. He began by trying to uncover the truth behind the mysterious death of a former student council president on Geomun Island during the military regime, a pursuit that led him into anti-government activities under a guise of company employment in an attempt to help employees of small companies organize labor union against employer. Later, as the director of the Solidarity for People's Solidarity for Participatory Democracy, he couldn't focus on literature and ended up far from the writing career he had envisioned. Thanks to him, however, I was able to explore literature through the works he introduced me to, such as Shin Dong-yup Biography, The Shell is Gone, and writings by Kim Won-il. I also discovered Aje Aje Bara Aje by Han Seung-won, the father of Han Kang, the 2024 Nobel Laureate in Literature. These works significantly deepened my literary understanding.

I worked in banking field until my early forties, then immigrated, always thinking of writing as an unreachable goal. Contributing monthly articles to the *Korea Times America* was my way of sharing my thoughts, hoping to connect with readers. Six years later, here I am, with a published book—a collection of nearly 70 essays. The feeling is surreal. I've practically memorized each piece I submitted, yet I know that readers don't retain every article, much like beads waiting to be strung into something more lasting. Binding them into a book has given me a deeper attachment to my work.

With my articles neatly organized online, I approached major Korean publishers, only to find no interest. I reached out to a Pechin (female), meaning friend on Facebook, who is a graduate of Saint Paul Girls' High School and have a oversea living experience at Singapore, inspired me. Through her, I was introduced to a publisher who had helped her publish her own book, opening the door for me to embark on my own publishing journey.

She'd recently published *Holding the Planet in Your Heart* with Kyunghee University professor Lee Man-yeol who is a American naturalized citizen in S. Korea. When she introduced me to her publisher, things moved quickly, almost as if destined. By the year's end, after completing a long-awaited project, I could cover the publishing costs. Amidst the holiday excitement, I spent meaningful time editing the manuscript and exchanging design ideas with the publisher, savoring every late night that brought me closer to this reality.

I owe a tremendous debt of gratitude to the editor in chief at *The Hankook Ilbo, aka The Korea Times America,* for their inspirational input on the book's design and devoted a valuable space of the paper to allow my article to be posted. I'm deeply thankful to those who attended the launch despite pandemic concerns, demonstrating genuine trust and solidarity. Special thanks go to the Bay Area community leaders who shared heartfelt congratulatory messages, the columnist and cellist who enriched the event with a moving cello performance, and the vice president lady of alumni association, who served as emcee with refreshing energy. The Mountain

View Church of the Seventh-day Adventist Church deserves my sincere appreciation as well for generously hosting the ceremony and providing so many conveniences. Their kindness and support truly made this event unforgettable.

Galaxy Express 999

2022-04-02 (sat)

"The blue horizon, white clouds flowing~"—this song, a cover by singer Park Jae-ran released in 1965, a year before I started school, became a tune I hummed as I grew up. Hawaii seemed as distant as heaven, a place I believed I would never reach, so I let the dream fade quickly. But "Pearly Shells," a Hawaiian nursery rhyme that celebrates the island paradise, lingers as one of the most beautiful songs in the world to me.

With vacation season drawing near and Waikiki's white sandy beaches calling, I wonder if it's finally time to visit again. It's been nearly 30 years since I first stopped by there on my way back from a two-month training program in New York while I was working at a bank in Korea. Now, I just want to live fully—work hard, travel often, and check items off my bucket list alongside meaningful people. As long as my body can carry me, I feel compelled to go, to explore.

"Are you vertical?" Americans ask. It's a greeting that touches on health—are you well and standing upright? When sickness hits, or one is confined to bed, that "horizontal" life begins, transforming the simple word into a poignant image, laden with the weight of confinement. That word, "horizontal," which opens with lightness, turns into a gravity-laden reality that speaks to the end of our days.

Yesterday, I stopped by her social media wall to let her know that I had published a book, recalling how, two years ago, I had bought two volumes of her essay collection. I'd always thought of her as someone who had it all—a doctor husband, a secure and happy life. But now, she's in intensive care, facing a barrage of tests. The breast cancer she thought she'd beaten two years ago has returned and metastasized throughout her body, forcing her to start putting her affairs in order with the time she has left. The gravity of the news left me solemn, and all I could manage was a simple message, hoping for a 'miraculous recovery.'

Death—the one subject everyone tries to avoid. Just as people around the world were beginning to breathe a little easier, putting aside the constant specter of death that COVID-19 cast over us, another crisis emerged. Ukraine, a nation of 48 million with a landmass three times that of the Korean Peninsula, has been plunged into turmoil. A month has passed since Putin's Russia, eager to showcase its might, launched an invasion, leaving the country devastated and countless people dead. Nearly three million Ukrainians have fled, seeking safety in neighboring nations. The loss of innocent lives and the forced displacement of so many are undeniable war crimes against humanity. While a handful argue that Ukraine somehow provoked this and now faces the consequences, anyone of sound mind condemns this violence, seeing Putin's actions as nothing less than diabolical.

Reflecting on the fragility of life—whether at the hands of illness or senseless violence—forces us to confront that unspoken topic.

Didn't Hitler and the war-hungry forces of Japanese imperialism, blinded by their own delusions of grandeur, ultimately face tragic downfalls? Obsessed with frenzied wars, ignoring widespread condemnation, these leaders either shot themselves in the head or met disgraceful ends at war crime trials. Reflect on this: as you relax in a warm apartment in winter, maybe even watching 'Gayo Stage (means Golden Oldies in Korean Language)' with announcer Kim Dong-gun, who's been an icon for decades, imagine a rock suddenly crashing through your living room. It's shocking enough in a peaceful space; how much more horrific to face the constant fear of shells exploding around you, transforming homes into living hells where no one can survive.

No matter how history is interpreted, Putin and Russia's actions—invading sovereign territory and stripping a neighboring country's right to choose its own fate—are nothing short of neighborhood thuggery on an international scale. Whether Putin steps down or withdraws troops, the world needs to see this conflict end. My heartfelt wish is for lasting peace to settle over Ukraine, a land deserving stability and safety for its people.

Reading a heartbreaking post from a friend on Facebook about their father's struggles in a nursing home stirred a familiar ache in my heart. The father had been admitted to a hospital in Gwangju for manageable care, yet due to COVID restrictions, he endured nearly two years without proper family visits, leaving him unable to voice his grievances.

The post described the unfair and unkind treatment he suffered, despite the hefty monthly fee of 1 million won equaling to $800—a sobering reminder of the challenges families face in ensuring quality care for their loved ones.

Even more distressing was how the staff intimidated him into silence, preventing him from speaking out against their service—an appalling violation of his right to freedom of speech and expression.

Knowing that his final days were marked by loneliness, frustration, and a lack of dignity makes this tragedy all the more devastating.

Reflecting on this, I feel a renewed determination to live meaningfully with my loved ones, maintaining bonds that bring joy and respect and striving to ensure that my final days are ones of peace and dignity. Taking a glance at my own selfie from the shoreline yesterday, I notice myself smiling, quietly pondering life's fleeting nature. Though my weight fluctuates and has now settled back around 220 pounds, I still feel strong and upright, facing life with a sense of purpose. In the end, I wonder: will I pass in the warmth of an embrace, a silent farewell, or drift off peacefully in my sleep? When my body is tossed into the firepit of the creamery, would I get up back to life out of too much fire heat inside? If there's a next life/world, maybe a star beyond where the Galaxy Express 999 travels, will I leave any lingering regrets behind?

Oh, the Grand Canyon!

2022-05-07 (sat)

"Oh wow~ That kid is really good at studying Korean history...How admirable,'" my aunt, a retired elementary school teacher now living in Jinhae at the age of ninety, would say whenever she remembered the young, spirited nephew Youngjae, my sister's son . His enthusiasm for history had left a lasting impression on her, even after all these years.

This year, for the first time ever, my two older sisters and I embarked on a 2,000-mile journey across the United States. Our adventure took us from San Francisco to Los Angeles, Las Vegas, the Grand Canyon, and Death Valley. For years, I had been encouraging my sisters—now 69 and 66, living in Gimhae and Yangsan—to explore the U.S. with me, and at last, we made it happen.

Finally, I managed to bring this long-held dream to life. Over the course of our 11-night, 12-day family trip, we stumbled upon memories we had tucked away, each recollection like a leaf in the recesses of our minds. These rediscoveries felt priceless, stirring up feelings that couldn't be replaced.

My immediate older sister and her husband (my

nephew's father) often engaged in playful banter, each throwing out absurd remarks. She would sometimes dismiss him with a teasing comment like, "You're not from a decent family!"

One day, this habit sparked a moment of brilliance from my nephew, who was in fifth grade at the time. Siding with his father, he quipped, *"What's so great about the Gyeongsan Kim family? They're descendants of Eunseolgong, the third son of the last King Gyeongsun—the one who ruined Silla!"*

His unexpected historical reference caught them all off guard, leaving them momentarily speechless.

After our Ensenada cruise in Mexico, we headed for Las Vegas, relished a hearty breakfast, and soon disembarked. The three of us—survivors of the cold, hungry days in the poor hillside village of Donam-dong in the '60s and '70s—now bonded together in our 60s and 70s here in the United States, set off straight for our stay at the MGM Park Hotel in Las Vegas. To pass the time on the five-hour drive, I teased my immediate older sister, my longtime rival during our teenage years, about it being a "miracle" that her children were even born, given how much she'd been my sworn enemy back then. She laughed and came back with her own banter.

At that moment, I found myself wishing our mother could be with us and reflecting on my eldest sister, who is six years older than me. If our mother were still alive, she would be 96, and I imagined her with the strength and energy for a trip like this. Looking at my eldest sister, I was struck by how much she resembles our mother when she was 70.

As we drove on, I imagined my mother riding along, still

lively and vibrant. Suddenly, a memory surfaced, pulling me back 26 years to 1996. That year, we celebrated my mother's 70th birthday at the Sky Lounge of a hotel across from Jobang (Chosun Textile) in Beomil-dong near Busan Station.

Gripping the steering wheel, I stole a glance beside me and caught sight of my eldest sister—now the age my mother once was—sitting in the passenger seat. It had been seven or eight years since I last dreamt of my mother, yet in that moment, she felt so present, almost as if she were there with us once more.

Yes, now that I think about it, my older sister truly does resemble our mother.

After my father's business took a downturn, my mom, who had been used to the comfortable life in the affluent Dongdaeshin-dong area of Busan, had to adjust to the sudden hardships of our new life in the hilly village of Donam-dong. My mother, who even sold American goods which she purchased Namdaemun Goblin Market to resell among neighbor, had always approached life with serenity, but my spirited oldest sister—who did she inherit that from, I wonder?

On our way to Las Vegas, we made a stop at the Hannam Chain Market in Diamond Bar. I showed my sisters around this bustling market, familiar to so many local Korean Americans. We had some Jajangmyeon (famous Korean black noodles) (noodles in black bean sauce) at the food court and packed the cooler with ice before resuming our enjoyable drive. We reached the majestic Hoover Dam in Arizona by evening, just beyond our hotel in Vegas.

The dam, a testament to engineering and perseverance,

was constructed over five years from 1931 under the guidance of Republican President Hoover, a Stanford-educated engineer, as part of the New Deal. The fact that it was built nearly 90 years ago, yet stands so modern and enduring, is astonishing. Reflecting on it, I'm reminded how history isn't just stories—it's right here before us, embodied in structures like this. Not long after its completion, in 1941, Japanese forces would launch their surprise attack on Pearl Harbor, and less than a decade later, in 1949, the Nationalist government under Chiang Kai-shek would be forced to flee to Taiwan, defeated by Mao Zedong's Communist forces.

As evening descended, and with the crowds still thin before peak vacation season, we wandered on top of the Hoover Dam, snapping a few photos in the chilly wind that swept across our faces. Later, we returned to Vegas, where we warmed up with a hearty meal of spicy pollack stew and bottle of makgeolli, a traditional rice wine and Pajeon, a green onion Pancake at a Korean restaurant on the main strip. That night, we checked into our hotel and quickly fell asleep, resting up for the next day's adventure—the Grand Canyon, the top destination on my bucket list.

The next morning, we began the challenging five-hour drive to the Grand Canyon—ten hours round trip for someone like me, not too fond of long-distance driving. Before exploring the canyon, we stopped at a picnic area, where we grilled pork belly purchased the day before at Hannam Chain Market, shared a soju toast, and cooked Shin Ramen and coffee while reminiscing about our childhood.

My mother used to sit on a rock overlooking the hill across from the rice shop at the entrance of Shinhungsa Temple, waiting until the shop was empty of customers. Only then, with quiet hesitation, would she finally gather the courage to enter.

My sisters told me how she would shyly step inside to ask the shop owner—the father of my elementary school friend, Kyungchul—for rice on credit, enduring the hardship with silent dignity to feed us. As we recalled this memory, we all sighed, feeling the weight of h

r sacrifices.

Standing before the Grand Canyon—a sight we had only seen in photos—felt surreal. The vastness of the landscape before us was humbling, much like the depth of our mother's resilience and love.

As the Honam-born young comedian, Kim Byung-man, joked in his famous skit, "If you haven't been there, don't talk about it!"

If we'd had more time, we could have stayed in a canyon-area hotel, gone trekking, and fully absorbed the landscape's majesty. But instead, we had to return for a show we'd booked in Vegas. Rather than feeling regret, we decided to view it as a promise to return someday.

My sisters, unfamiliar with casinos, were completely taken with the experience. I, too, had hoped for a bit of jackpot luck over breakfast, but it wasn't meant to be. Instead, fortune smiled on me when I won $500 on a scratch-off ticket I picked up at a gas station enroute to Death Valley. It felt as if the heavens were showing a little favor to me and my sisters, here in America for the first time.

My dear sisters, may you stay healthy and live long.

The Dobermann of Half Moon Bay

2023-05-12 (Sat)

On a bright Sunday morning, my eyes stung as the sunlight streamed in, and I lazily reached for my smartphone. Where should I spend my day today? Last night, I found myself frustrated and weighed down by a remark made by a friend from my elementary school BAND, an online alumni SNS. He's been in the U.S. for 35 years, , which is 10 years longer period than me, yet his words had the strange power to bother me deeply. Another friend, chiming in with a dismissive, "Why are you angry?" felt like an unwanted mediator, as if trying to ease things like an interfering sister-in-law.

Living here as an immigrant without any real bragging rights, sometimes I also feel like saying, "Hey, look at these achievements," just to prove to others that I've carved something to brag about out of this immigrant life. Unfortunately, I can't find anything worthwhile that I can brag about. But when I heard him say, "Well, you wouldn't really understand, having lived in the U.S. for such a short time," something in me flared up. I was, strangely, far too quick-tempered lately, with my defense mechanisms ready to jump in: "Hey, excuse me, what did you just say?" Of course, I should have held back. It's not like people haven't told me I don't know much before. So, what was it about this comment that got under my skin?

Reflecting on it now, I'm reminded of how challenging it truly is to embody the spirit of someone like Dosan Ahn Chang-ho. He was a revered leader who, a hundred years ago, tried to reason with Korean ginseng vendors in downtown San Francisco. They were fighting over the rights to sell their wares, sometimes even passing off Chinese ginseng as Korean to secure sales, and Dosan would step in, intervening like a mediator between friends, trying to instill a sense of integrity and unity. How simple it sounds, but how difficult it is to live up to that spirit of understanding and patience.

I took a deep breath and reflected on what happened the night before.

This friend of mine was someone I remembered from elementary school—strong-willed, always the top dog, and deeply devout. He played soccer with the skill of Eusébio, yet despite his talent and confidence, he never bullied those with gentler spirits. Over the years, I often wondered where life had taken him and how he had grown.

When he reappeared in my life last year, claiming that he had also immigrated to the U.S. and joined a BAND, it was the first time I had seen him online in fifty years. As it turned out, the comment that had irked me so much was merely an awkward joke—his attempt to lighten the mood.

Having been away from Korea for so long, he had lost the finer nuances in his words, and his clumsy attempt at humor backfired, creating a misunderstanding. Hey Ji-seong from Tennessee!, if you're reading this, I'm truly sorry for my own narrow-mindedness and overreaction.

Yet, it remains true that some people really know how to push the buttons. This brings to mind an incident from some time ago on a bright spring day. I was walking along the serene beach at Half Moon Bay—a hidden gem, not widely known. As I wandered along the water's edge, my eyes caught sight of a winding flower-laden staircase leading up the cliffside along the Pacific coast. I was enchanted. Ignoring the "No Trespassing" sign, I hummed to myself, "What could happen? Who hasn't broken a rule or two for beauty?" I climbed the steps slowly, my gaze following a little yellow butterfly that seemed to be guiding me. Soon, a wide, open grassy field unfolded before me atop the cliff, and I was rewarded with the cool, refreshing sea breeze—a private moment of bliss, just me and the vast sky.

Out of nowhere, a ferocious Dobermann suddenly appeared, charging at me with a terrifying intensity. The grumpy old man, clearly waiting to catch intruders, released the dog, allowing it to lunge straight toward me. Oh no! Though my heart pounded in fear, I held my ground, meeting the dog's gaze with a steely stare and managing, somehow, to subdue it with what I can only describe as a flash of instinctive resolve.

As the old man approached, he told me I could either return the way I came or pay a $5 toll to continue. I had come too far to retreat meekly, so I muttered, "Annoying old man," under my breath. I handed over the toll and walked the long path back to California Highway 1. The memory of that day still lingers as one of the worst experiences I've ever had—it makes my stomach turn just recalling it.

After folding the laundry, I took it from the dryer, prepared for the week's clothing, and set off down the sunlit road, heading to the Shoreline Beach Trail. Unlike that day, this place always greets me warmly, filling me with peace.

Nothing Lasts Forever

2022-06-11 (sat)

The alumni association newsletter from my alma mater, typically released around the 5th of each month, was due on the 9th, but I hadn't seen anything yet. Curious, I reached out to Director Choi at the Seoul office, who assured me it would be available soon, albeit a few days late. For the past four years, I've been honoredho to serve as the president of the San Francisco Bay Area alumni association. It's been my pleasure to regularly forward the newsletter to local alumni—seniors and juniors alike—through email and KakaoTalk messanger.

There's a unique joy in staying connected to the institution that shaped us, instilling knowledge, humanity, and character, enabling us to establish ourselves and grow steadily in this foreign land. Sometimes, I've sent out news updates so frequently that it might have bordered on annoying someone, and I initiated an annual development fund drive, contributing some of the proceeds back to our alma mater in the form of scholarships. Despite a hectic schedule, I managed to complete my term with no major issues.

Last March, I had the good fortune to pass the leadership to a highly capable 16 years junior alumni, who has been working in IT consulting here in Silicon Valley. Seeing this generational shift gives me hope that younger alumni, who may have felt somewhat disconnected, will now find renewed interest and involvement. Some seniors expressed mild disappointment over my departure, as they'd grown accustomed to my communication style, but that's life, isn't it? When it's time to step down, one must. After all, nothing in this world is forever.

Ding! Director Choi sent me another KakaoTalk message, and when I opened it, I was greeted by a familiar yet sorrowful image of a street. At age 95... "National MC Song Hae, who hosted the *National Singing Contest* for 35 years since 1988 and was recently registered in the Guinness Book of World Records as the oldest TV music competition program host, passed away yesterday." The photo showed the funeral home set up on a street in Nakwon-dong, Seoul, with his bust, and it seemed as though even the sky was mourning, as crowds gathered in the rain to pay their respects.

Seeing his age—95—makes it easy to acknowledge that he lived a long life. Still, his passing feels so sudden. Just ten days ago, we'd heard he was hospitalized, and everyone believed he'd soon recover, leave his sickbed, and maybe even return to entertain us. If he couldn't return to broadcasting, surely he'd be consulting with the station about choosing a successor. Yet, life had other plans.

This reminds me again of how fragile life is. We can never know when or how we might leave, yet we often live as if we're here forever. I feel compelled to live beautifully, to appreciate each day, openly sharing with good people, supporting and cherishing them—even missing them, in a sense, while they're still right here.

Although Song Hae was a friendly supporting actor

alongside some of the greatest comedians of his time, like Koo Bong-seo and Bae Sam-ryong, his life was marked by unimaginable hardships. It wasn't until he became the MC of the *National Singing Contest* in 1988, at age 61, that he achieved widespread recognition. Yet, even then, he carried the sorrow of losing his only son in a car accident. Reflecting on his life, I think of him as a lone pine tree by a creek, resilient with moss covering its back—a symbol of endurance and quiet strength amid life's trials.

I admit it's easy to be a fan of celebrities like Jeon In-hwa or Yano Shiho, the wife of MMA fighter Choo Sung-hoon, aka Yoshihiro Akiyama, nicknamed as 'Sexyyama, yet when I heard from my sisters about how mom, who passed away about a decade ago, had been a devoted fan of Mr. Song Hae, I understood why. For over 60 years, Mr. Song Hae reportedly left his home in Dogok-dong Gangnam daily, commuting by bus and subway to his office in Nakwon-dong, where he would enjoy a modest bowl of noodles at his favorite soup spot for just 2,000 won equivalent $2.

That stretch of Nakwon-dong, with its rice cake shop, instrument store, and the Hollywood Theater, evokes memories of my younger days, sneaking into a movie screening at 19, barely daring to breathe during Olivia Hussey and Leonard Whiting's famous kiss in *Romeo and Juliet.*

Just three years ago, I had the privilege of visiting that very hangover soup shop and paying my respects to the Song Hae's bust nearby. Now, as his iconic call of "Nationwide, singing contest! Ding-dong-daeng-dong-daeng. can no longer fill the air, it's a sorrow felt by many. Although separated by the Pacific, I bow before his spirit in my heart, grateful for the joy he brought us. May you rest in peace, sir. We were truly blessed to share so many years with you.

Giants of Silicon Valley's Korean Community

2022-07-23 (Sat)

Silicon Valley's Korean community is home to many prominent figures in the cultural and artistic circles. Previously, I introduced respected novelist Ms. Shin Yeasun, who achieved remarkable success with her full-length novel *Etranger, where is your Hometown?*, published in 1966. This work not only became a bestseller but was also recognized as one of the "30 best Korean Novels" by KBS Radio in 1985, earning a spot in the special feature "Novel Theater," which endeared her to many Koreans.

Today, I want to spotlight Ms. Eun-ju Park, a multifaceted talent as a novelist, playwright, filmmaker, and the founder and president of both the 'Eun-ju Park Sprout Literature Society' and the 'Silicon Valley Writer's Group.' She also serves as the president of the Shinsaimdang Association and remains passionately active in her pursuits, even in her mid-80s.

Meeting Ms. Park feels like encountering a giant who has surmounted barriers that many deem insurmountable. She has authored five or six outstanding books, including the autobiographical novel Confession (1995), which deeply resonates with both the Korean immigrant experience and the lives of people in Korea. These works are far more than ordinary stories—they have the power to profoundly move and inspire readers.

As you read the book, you'll naturally uncover the honored novelist senior lady's remarkable life story. Born to a Japanese father who was a pilot in the Japanese Navy and lost his life during the Pacific War, and a Korean mother, her journey back to Korea with her mom after the war was filled with challenges. During her childhood, she faced teasing from friends, who called him a "Jjokbari" meaning Japs. This experience echoes the themes found in the late Pak Kyongni's historical novel *Land*, where a character weeps quietly in the bamboo forest behind Choi Cham-pan's house in Hadong at midnight.

One poignant moment in the narrative occurs when Gucheon-i (Kim Hwan), born out of wedlock after a secret rape by Kim Gae-ju—a Donghak jeopju, a leader of famers rebellion group escaped to mountian temple from Jeongeup—struggles with his unrequited love for Byeoldang assi (Byeoldang lady) the wife (sister-in-law) of Choi Chi-su, the head of Choi Cham-pan's household. His anguish is reminiscent of a shock I experienced when I was twenty.

After publishing just one volume of essays that were serialized in the *Hankook Ilbo, aka The Korea Times America, aka The Korea Times America* for six years, I sometimes feel a sense of arrogance. Yet, those who have authored multiple novels and passionately strive to enlighten overseas Koreans operate on a different level, inspiring profound respect within me.

Recently, I learned online that her husband had passed away after a battle with cancer. I went to offer my condolences, and she graciously presented me with a new book containing her works, which I gratefully accepted. These two individuals are truly giants in their fields.

There is one thing I regret not taking a more ambitious step in: running, which I have enjoyed as a hobby throughout my life. I started with half marathons and decided to run a full course, but in the end, I never completed a full marathon, and my knees have suffered as a result.

I think it was around 1992 when I was in my early thirties that I participated in several half marathons, including the Seorak Half Marathon, completing a total of six. However, I never ran a full marathon after that due to various excuses life threw my way. If I had to compare it to a full course marathon, I would say that the 25-kilometer race held on the rugged mountains of Bul-am san and Surak-san at the Northen suburb of Seoul in 1993 was quite the challenge. I finished it in 4 hours and 55 minutes, breaking the 5-hour time limit. At that time, I was so exhausted from going up and down the last ridge that I felt I might have a near-death experience. The moment I finally crossed the finish line and collapsed on the mountain path, I realized that my big left toenail had fallen off while I was catching my breath in the sauna in Junggye-dong after the race.

I have lived my whole life regretting, "I should have challenged myself to run the full marathon from the beginning." The adage, "Boys, be ambitious!" still serves as a reminder to keep striving when I find myself becoming lax.

Vancouver...From Delay to Delight

2022-09-03 (Sat)

Oh no, this can't be happening.

I left the office with plenty of time to spare, planning to arrive two hours early for my first flight to Vancouver. Just as I was about to leave, I suddenly had to sign some important paperwork for the California Department of Real Estate. After stopping by UPS to get it done, I finally made my way to San Francisco airport.

Once I parked in the long-term lot, I took the dedicated train for another 20 minutes to International Terminal 1. When I arrived in a hurry, I saw that there were only 30 minutes left until takeoff, but I couldn't find the airline desk, no matter how much I looked around while dragging my suitcase to check in. Eventually, I stumbled upon a desk in a dim corner with no lights on, only to be told by the staff that check-in had already closed.

Oh my... I had been eagerly anticipating this trip for months, excited to reunite with my fellow Vancouver alumni and classmates I met on the Mexico cruise last May. Now, it felt as if I was sitting in a darkened auditorium after the final act of a play, drained of all strength and enveloped in a sense of despair.

Oh, what is this... A young Indian friend, who found himself in a similar situation, kindly helped me buy Air Canada flight tickets for a flight three hours later, as if it were his own business. We barely managed to arrive in Vancouver around midnight.

Hong, my close 2 years senior alumni pal, who had recently stepped down as the president of the Vancouver area Alumni Association after four years, was waiting for me at that late hour. He is a close senior with five overlapping experiences: college, major, Air Force officer, working at the headquarters of the Korea Exchange Bank. I learned much later that he had spent time reading a collection of world classics at the Namsan City Library while waiting for his immigration visa to Canada, where his wife awaited his arrival, eating cheap Udon or Curry & Rice for lunch at the cafeteria, which was exactly same sequence of events that I was in right before him, waiting for my US visa to immigrate to San Francisco 20 years ago.

I must have thought of Vancouver as if it were just another American city. However, it was a neighboring country I could only reach by taking an international flight. Although my trip lasted just two nights and three days, I arrived late at night and was deeply captivated by Vancouver's beautiful people and stunning scenery. Canada is a social welfare state where guns are prohibited, similar to Korea, so society feels very peaceful. Medical expenses and education up to high school are free, but how can Vancouver be so beautiful?

Having lived a lonely life in a foreign land like the United States, with few people to share my joys and sorrows, I was deeply moved by the thrill of traveling to a place where people genuinely wanted to meet me and were eagerly waiting for my arrival.

Campus couple juniors alumni from Dallas, whom I met again three months after the cruise in May, brought along their son, Haneul, a former Princeton University football player (offensive center) who now works in Seattle, a neighboring border city. The evening I arrived, they were scheduled to demonstrate how to make kimchi for their son's American neighbors in Seattle, so they had to turn around and leave after only spending half a day with them at Lions Park in Coquitlam.

Their eyes soon became moist with regret at parting from their beloved alumni. Witnessing the warm hospitality of Vancouver alumni, who willingly carried our heavy loads from all over the U.S., prepared parties, grilled barbecue and green onion pancakes, and joyfully guided us to tourist attractions made me feel that Vancouver was the most wonderful place in the world, inhabited by the most beautiful people. Vancouver is a place where individuals readily roll up their sleeves, work together, and cultivate affectionate relationships. How heavenly it is! I want to go and live there right now.

Reflections on Hangul Day

2022-10-08 (Sat)

In October, Korea celebrates a series of significant days: Armed Forces Day on the 1st, National Foundation Day on the 3rd, and Hangeul Day on the 9th, marking the 576th anniversary of the creation of Hangeul. This remarkable achievement was made possible when King Sejong the Great gathered scholars from the Royal Academy to conduct research.

Forty-seven years ago, in 1975, I entered high school located in front of Dongdaemun Baseball Stadium, where I experienced several fresh shocks and impressions. One standout memory was how seniors, just one year my elder, would visit each class during break time to introduce their special activity groups and invite us freshmen to join. As expected of a commercial school, seniors from various special activity groups, such as abacus, book-keeping, gardening, literature, and band, would enthusiastically present their activities, capturing our interest.

What surprised me was how someone only a year older could deliver such impressive presentations on stage. One presentation that remains vivid in my memory was by a senior from the 'Korean Language Preservation Movement' club. Although it was nearly half a century ago and I don't recall every word he spoke, his passionate plea to reject foreign languages as much as possible and to preserve our precious Korean language resonated deeply with me. He emphasized the importance of protecting our beautiful Hangeul, created by King Sejong, from the overwhelming influx of foreign words at the time. I honestly found it hard to contain my surprise; it was truly amazing.

Now that almost fifty years have passed, I find myself reflecting on the nature of language. Language is a system of transmission of things and ideas that originates from the place where civilization began. Therefore, even when we encounter foreign words, we must consider how challenging and wasteful it is to forcefully create and spread them in Hangeul. In the midst of a tsunami of new civilizations, including the Internet, fabless technology, system semiconductors, smartphones, electric cars, SpaceX rockets, and asteroid spacecraft crash tests, etc., striving to exclusively express all of these concepts in Hangeul may leave us exhausted before we can even keep pace with rapidly developing civilization.

Instead, I believe it would be more meaningful to work towards the globalization of Korean culture by promoting our exceptional achievements—such as kimchi, K-pop, and K-dramas like *Squid Game*—so that other countries may naturally follow suit.

Moreover, even without recalling reports from several years ago about a remote Indonesian village deciding to use Hangeul as its official alphabet, the fact that Hangeul is an excellent writing system is an objective truth with considerable persuasive power both domestically and internationally, extending beyond simple self-satisfaction.

However, despite its strengths, there are questions about whether Hangeul is an infallible writing system that needs no improvement. We must approach the fact that there are many foreign words that cannot be accurately represented in Hangeul with an open mind. For instance, letters such as "th," "f," and "r" in English have no direct equivalents in Hangeul. Is the word "thread," which always follows a needle, truly "thread" or should it be written as "tre-d"?

> Thread – 쓰레드x, 뜨레드x, ㅼ레드o
> Rice- 라이스(lice)x, 롸이스o
> Face- 페이스x, 헤이스x, ᄅᆌ이스o
> Star- 스타x, 스타̌o

Of course, this is merely a suggestion for foreign language notation, but even small improvements could significantly reduce the limitations of what Hangeul can express and, conversely, greatly expand its communicative power. Ahead of the 576th Hangeul Day, I quietly offer this suggestion from San Francisco, across the Pacific Ocean, as I reflect on the potential for growth and adaptation in our cherished language.

Chapter 9
Barefoot Isadora

The Korean Chipmunk of Las Vegas

2022-11-26 (Sat)

"I knew if I stayed around long enough, something like this would happen." This sentiment echoed the famous epitaph of the renowned Irish playwright George Bernard Shaw. When this event was announced last August, I should have made a reservation in advance. However, I hesitated, weary of the "just in case" mentality, and only two days before, I hurriedly bought a golden time ticket from San Jose on a Friday, ultimately having to pay for a flight to Korea on a newly launched airline as much as for the flight to Korea on a newly launched airline.

Not a single animal, not even an insect, was visible. After climbing for two hours along a mountain path densely packed with five-leaf pines and fir trees, We finally reached Cathedral Rock, 2,625 meters above sea level. It's almost as high as Baekdusan Mountain. Don't be surprised to learn that Mount Charleston Peak, which seemed within arm's reach to the west, requires another four hours of climbing. This peak is about 12,000 feet high, comparable to Japan's highest peak, Mt. Fuji, falling short by only 150 meters. It's astonishing that such a high mountain exists in Las

Vegas.

Although it was only a three-mile round trip climb that We began after driving to an elevation of 2,000 meters, I realized I had already reached the highest altitude of my life. When I was an 18-year-old college freshman, I had only climbed Daecheongbong (1,708 m, or 5608ft) on Seoraksan Mountain once with two of my elementary school classmates. I had never been to Baeknokdam (1,947 m, or 6387ft) on Hallasan Mountain or Cheonwangbong (1,915 m, or 6282ft) on Jirisan Mountain. I was a total newbie, and I had never reached a peak. Still, I was able to summit after navigating the mountain path while leaning on the hiking sticks that our host, Senior Choi, had carefully prepared for us in advance and chatting about this and that.

The previous day, in the middle of the desert, the only living things I could see were a grasshopper, two small mice, and a few dwarf shrubs standing here and there, showcasing their tenacity for life. I went hiking in Valley of Fire State Park, a barren landscape of red rock formations where I could see Elephant Rock, sculpted into the shape of an elephant by thousands of years of weathering, and Indian petroglyphs etched into a 30-meter-high cliff. I felt a thrill at the traces of the civilization that once thrived here thousands of years ago, spread out before my eyes, transcending time and space.

Skitter-skatter... As I looked down at the distant view below the mountains and the long, runway-like desert valley that seemed to be shrouded in a hazy yellow dust cloud for miles, I took a bite of the energy bar that my hostess, Mrs. Choi—renowned for her mountaineering skills and affectionately dubbed "Wonder Woman" during her time at Seoul National University's mountaineering club—had given me.

Suddenly, I noticed something crawling out of the crevices of the cliff. I looked up, and oh my! It resembled a baby Korean squirrel that someone had smuggled out and released. When I offered it some of my food, it quickly grabbed it and disappeared again. Though it looked like a baby, it was actually a fully grown adult—a type of squirrel known as a 'chipmunk.' Compared to the squirrels I remembered from home, this one was only half the size, but its face, along with the three or four black stripes extending from its neck to its tail, and its cute expression, were strikingly similar. The only difference was that, unlike the Korean squirrel's tail—which points skyward in the shape of a question mark—this adorable creature's tail was horizontal, almost brushing the ground.

After the hike, we stopped by the Wynn Hotel, a famous casino in Vegas. An alumna, an expert in blackjack, won $400 in just 20 minutes and boldly got up from her seat, leaving a deep impression on the seven participants by treating us all to a hotel buffet. After spending three days in Las Vegas, I realized that it was a truly amazing place. Why do I feel captivated by every place I visit and want to settle down and live there? It must be because I am a country bumpkin who doesn't know much about the world.

A Rabbit in the Rain

2023-01-28 (Sat)

'This wasn't taken on a cruise~'

She, a well-known real estate agent in Orange County, shared a photo in an alumni KakaoTalk chat room—a cruise ship floating on the blue horizon, with white clouds drifting past the window. I said it looked like it was taken on a cruise for Ensenada, Mexico which we went together during alumni reunion event, but in reality, it was snapped at a quiet café in Huntington Beach, where she arrived after running south along the 21-mile 'Beach Boulevard' under the clear blue sky.

The heavy rain wasn't limited to the San Francisco Bay Area. After all, the worst winter rains in 162 years since the Great Flood of 1861-62 have finally subsided, leaving the streets so fluffy that you can hardly tell it rained, except for the branches hanging over the gutters.

At the end of last year, with the harsh reality of the pandemic and the unusually heavy rainfall, emotions ran high as another year came to a close. However, already in late January, there were numerous reports about compatriots and neighbors who had turned their backs on this world or tragically lost their lives along with their entire families, or to the bullets of robbers, and my heart still aches. What is more precious than life? No matter how cornered I felt and how overwhelmed by despair I was, why did I have to abandon this world so vainly without even thinking of asking for help?

With a pen in my mouth, I look out the window of my fourth-floor office at the cloudy sky and momentarily lose myself in thought.

The winter monsoon season that I had been waiting for passed like this. Just as I took a breath, the commercial deal that had been dragging on for five months was finally completed when the client received SBA loan funding. This case involved a lucrative cash flow business with an annual net income of over $500,000.

It was a package deal of a property and business on it, the process from loan application to funding was a complicated journey that would have tested.

The amount of data that had to be submitted was nearly as extensive as writing a master's thesis, if not a doctoral one. I am truly grateful to the customer for their steadfastness throughout the entire process.

Last week, the Lunar New Year of the Rabbit, which the state of California designated as a new holiday starting this year, passed. This year marks the 72nd birthday of my eldest sister-in-law, born in 1951, the Year of the Rabbit. She married to my eldest brother to join our family about 40 years ago but sadly lost her husband (my older brother) to become a widow ten years ago.

The Year 2022, also known as the year of Im-in Tiger, was one of the best years of my life. It is a lucky coincidence that my mother was born in the same Tiger year, 1926, who would be 97 this year.

Throughout our lives, there are days when the sun

shines, and this past year was exceptionally bright for me. I quietly became an author for the first time by publishing a book of essays that I had written over the past six years in the Korea Times America. Additionally, I was able to rekindle the precious love of family by inviting my two older sisters on a Mexican cruise, and we continued to tour Las Vegas, the Hoover Dam, the Grand Canyon, Death Valley, Universal Studios, and the Getty Museum. Witnessing my sisters' joy, like that of elementary school girls on a field trip, was a wonderful opportunity for me to reflect on our cherished family ties.

That's not all. Four years ago, when I encountered a problem with my knee, I felt discouraged and had to stop my weekend runs of 20 km. However, I was able to shake off that nightmare by dramatically resuming it through my regular self-rehabilitation.

Additionally, during a morning ritual in the bathroom one morning, I discovered the secret to completely recovering from hemorrhagic anemia, a chronic condition I had thought I would just live with indefinitely, by thinking out of the box and taking one more relaxing minute at the same time, which worked miraculously well.

I admit that sometimes when loneliness creeps in, I let out a long sigh without realizing it. However, overall, it has been a very fulfilling year, like a warm stone pot bibimbap mixed perfectly with sesame oil and gochujang. I couldn't be happier. What wonderful experiences await us in the Gye-myo new year of Rabbit?

Barefoot Isadora

2023-05-20 (Sat)

"Isadora, it's quite cold. Why not wear a cape in the open-air car?"
"No, worries, this long and beautiful silk scarf you gave me is enough. Bye! I am off to love…" Boohoo~.

One night in September 1927, nearly a hundred years ago, Isadora left us on the coastal road of Nice, France, leaving behind her last words. She passed away unexpectedly at just 50 years old. In a tragic turn of events, the scarf she wore around her neck was caught by the wind and entangled in the rear wheel of the car, tragically causing her to be thrown from the vehicle and resulting in a fatal neck injury.

I still vividly remember the joy of the day we first brought a record player into our home. It was around 1976 when I was in high school. At that time, expensive manufacturing brands like the Cheonilsa Byeolpyo record player were out of our reach, so I followed my oldest brother, who was 12 years older than me, to the Sewoon Plaza in Cheonggyecheon. After much bargaining, we bought an assembled product and carefully carried it home on the bus. Looking back, that day was one of the happiest days of my life.

I carefully placed the 8-track Paul Mauriat Orchestra music tape, the size of a lunchbox that shop owner had included as a bonus, into the cartridge. The most amazing stereo sound I had ever heard began to fill the room as "Love is Blue," "Toccata of Tears," and "El Bimbo" played. Soon, the unforgettable song "Barefoot Isadora" flowed out, moistening my heart. During my Sweet Sixteen teenage years, that song served as the theme for "Night Platform," a late-night youth radio show hosted by the popular voice actress Kim Se-won.

Ah, Isadora Duncan! No wonder the late Choi Seung-hee (1911-1969, aged 58), a legendary dancer who defected to North Korea and is now buried in the Patriotic Martyrs' Cemetery in Pyongyang, considered the forerunner of Joseon modern dance and a graduate of Sookmyung Girls' High School, is referred to as the Isadora Duncan of Joseon. She is still remembered by people to this day. I suddenly realize that the sorrowful melody I knew only by title is actually a tribute to the life of Isadora Duncan. Where else can you find such fluorescent lights?

Isadora Duncan (born 1877) is now very specific to me. First of all, she hails from San Francisco, where I have lived for 21 years since immigration. After her financier father and mother divorced, she moved to Oakland, cross the S.F. bay, with her mother. She taught dance to neighborhood girls while helping her mother with her sewing. When she was 20, she moved to New York and began to learn dance in earnest, developing her unique style. During the turbulent times around World War I, she moved to Europe and established dance schools in Berlin, London, and Moscow.

She broke away from the stereotypical costumes and movements of traditional ballet, drawing inspiration from the images of Greek reliefs in the British Museum. She gained worldwide fame by creating her own beautiful dance movements, wearing Greek-style ballet dresses designed by the famous designer Poiret, and dancing barefoot. It is quite fitting that the most prestigious award in the international dance world today is the "Isadora Duncan Award."

The second notable figure is choreographer Ong Kyung-il, a Korean dancer who served as a principal dancer at the National Dance Company of Korea in South Korea. After she immigrated to S.F., she built her own dance company called the Ong Dance Company and actively choreographed performances at the San Francisco Herbst Theater. She has won the Isadora Duncan Award twice. Four years ago, in 2019, we hosted a small congratulatory dinner party for her, attended by the late senior alumnus Mr. N and other distinguished guests.

Since then, however, many artists have faced significant challenges due to the pandemic, and there has been very little news about their performances or activities lately. This situation is deeply unfortunate for the San Francisco cultural scene and the Korean community, which often finds solace in the arts through exceptional performances. The difficulties caused by the pandemic extend beyond the performing arts, but as a fan, I remain hopeful that dancer Ong Kyung-il will return to the stage soon.

A Defector's Legacy-Captain Lee Woong-Pyeong

2023-09-02 (Sat)

"Wooo-OOOO-oooo-OOOO-oooo," I still vividly remember the tense situation on the morning of February 25, 1983—40 years ago—when the first real air raid warning swept across South Korea since the Korean War. Just 18 days later, I was set to enter the camp in the Air Force Training and Education Command as a member of the 78th officer candidate class.

As I learned about the horrors of the Korean War in elementary, middle, and high school, I would shudder at the thought of my predecessors who perished in brutal battles at places like the Chosin Reservoir during the freezing winter, at Baekmagoji, and along the Nakdong River front in Tabudong. They were shot by North Korean and Chinese soldiers, their youthful potential cut short before it had a chance to bloom. Now, was it finally our turn? I would bite my lip without realizing it.

About two years later, while serving as an intelligence officer at the ROKAF Combat Air Command, which located inside the US Osan Air Base for the 7th US Air Force. I was fortunate to catch the attention of Captain

Seo Kyung-hwan, a senior from the 75th class at the Air Force Headquarters who had been dispatched to Osan. He recommended me as the successor to his classmate, Captain Park Sung-hyun, who was due to be discharged from the headquarters at the same time as him. Luckily, I was transferred to the position of liaison officer for the Foreign Military Attachés in Korea at the Air Force Headquarters in Daebang-dong. Contrary to my expectations of being trained at the Nonsan Training Center and serving on the front lines as an Army infantryman, I found myself in a comfortable office complete with carpet, air conditioning, and a leather sofa, welcoming foreign military attachés.

One day in February 1986, just six months before my discharge, I was sitting on the sofa in my office, engaged in conversation with my immediate superior, Lieutenant Colonel Chang Young-gil. Suddenly, a tall, sturdy major with sharp eyes and a familiar face dropped by our office. It was Captain Lee Woong-pyeong, who had famously defected by piloting a MiG-19 fighter plane just before I entered in the basic officer candidates training camp, sending South Korea into a state of panic.

After defecting, Captain Lee was assigned to the 10th Fighter Squadron in Suwon and, in 1983, he received the largest defection reward in history at the time—an astonishing 1.5 billion won equivalent to $1.2 million. He became an intelligence officer in the Korean Air Force and later served as a policy researcher at the Air Force University. Enjoying his newlywed life in an Air Force apartment in Sindaebang-dong, he had married the daughter of an Air Force University professor. It was said that he often stopped by our military attaché liaison office whenever he had business at Air Force Headquarters, partly because Director Chang Young-gil had acted as an interrogator and mentor to Captain Lee after his defection, helping him adjust to life in South Korea.

As I greeted him and engaged in casual conversation, a real air raid warning suddenly blared across the country. This time, it was due to a Chinese Air Force J-6 bomber that had taken off from Shenyang and made an emergency landing in a rice paddy in Iksan, Jeollabuk-do. Captain Lee was immediately summoned to the Chief of Staff's office and asked me, "Lieutenant Kim, can you go to my house and bring me a pilot's uniform?"

I promptly drove to his residence, met Captain Lee's wife, explained the situation, and gave him the pilot's uniform. Captain Lee quickly changed his clothes and hurried up to the Chief of Staff's office. That was the last time I saw him, but I still vividly remember his dignified presence, with his sharp eyes and kind-hearted demeanor.

He had been married with two children in North Korea, was treated exceptionally well in South Korea and seemed to live happily. However, it is said that he succumbed to liver cirrhosis at the Armed Forces Capital Hospital in 2002, at the age of 48, after resorting to heavy drinking to cope with the stress of his life as a defector who had flown a MiG.

It has now been 21 years since he passed away, having lived his life as both a sacrificial lamb and a man of opportunity during a tumultuous era of division. Here in San Francisco, I took a moment to pray for the soul of the late Captain Lee Woong-pyeong, honoring his complex legacy and the sacrifices he made.

Happy Holidays in Chiang Mai!

2023-12-30 (Sat)

Mr. Elephant says his nose is his hand~
I took advantage of the Thanksgiving holiday to travel to Thailand and Taiwan for the first time in my life for two weeks. They say that elephants are the most gentle animals in the world, but who would have thought that I would be petting an elephant, feeding it a banana, and taking it to a stream to give it a bath?

We arrived at the Patara Elephant Farm, on board a public transportation in Chiang Mai to the farm, in a small pickup truck called a "tuk-tuk." This type of public transport has only an iron roof on the cargo bed and carries passengers for just one dollar for short distances and three dollars for longer ones. After learning some simple elephant commands, such as 'Soonpoong' (raise the trunk and open the mouth) and 'Didi' (patting the face—very good!), we began to interact with the elephants. They were thrilled when we picked bananas off the trees and fed them one by one. When I held out a banana, the elephant eagerly extended its trunk to take it, then gently licked my hand with its long trunk, asking for more.

Elephants are incredibly gentle, and since they eat all kinds of trees in the forest, there's no need to worry about the cost of their feed. While walking five elephants along with the keepers to a small river for their bath, I noticed the elephants straying from the path for a moment. They lifted their trunks, broke off small branches, and munched on them. Elephants consume about 150 kilograms of plants each day and can live an average of 60 years in the wild and up to 80 years in captivity. When fully grown, they can weigh about 5 tons, yet they are truly amazing animals that communicate so well with humans.

Finally, we arrived at a small river, and as the elephants lay down in the water with excitement, we gave them a refreshing bath using tree bark that naturally produced bubbles. Oh, the water was cold! At the keeper's command, the elephants filled their trunks with water and playfully sprayed us, making us scream with joy, much like the audience splashed by killer whales at Sea World in San Diego.

Chiang Mai, located in northern Thailand, is the country's second-largest city with a population of 1.2 million. It's also known as the hometown of former Prime Minister Thaksin Shinawatra. Though he is now in a jail due to corruption charges from his time in office, Thaksin, a former police officer who founded a successful mobile telecommunications company, rose to become one of Thailand's wealthiest individuals. At 52, he won a landslide victory in the 2001 general election, holding power for five years and becoming the first Thai prime minister in constitutional history to 'almost' complete a full term. He's remembered as a capable leader who elevated Thailand's standing.

It would be unreasonable to generalize about all of

Thailand from just a brief visit of 4 nights and 5 days, but the gentle, clean nature of Thai society stood out immediately. This seems to stem from the deeply rooted Buddhist culture, with its emphasis on meditation and alms-giving. I never saw anyone frowning or raising their voice; the entire atmosphere was calm and serene. Streets and markets alike were impressively clean, without a single piece of litter in sight.

Though Thailand's per capita income is much lower than Korea's, the tropical climate allows for three times more rice farming, ensuring that no one worries about hunger. Prices are also remarkably low: popular dishes like Pad Thai and Tom Yum Goong cost around $2 at food courts in department stores and just $1 at traditional markets. A comfortable two-bedroom condo can be had for as little as $40,000. Out of nowhere at the food court, I heard glowing reviews from retirees of the US and Europe, about my age, who were happily savoring their Tom Yum Goong.

In Thailand, bargaining is part of the experience—you can often buy something at a lower price by negotiating and pretending to walk away. But how much cheaper could one bargain when a two-hour Thai massage from a skilled, healthy 26-year-old therapist costs only $20? For five days straight, I enjoyed nearly daily two-hour massages, fully recharging and traveler's fatigue.

The Thai language is incredibly gentle and soft on the ears, much like French. The alphabet is round and beautiful, almost like a parade of elephants in written form. At the elephant farm, each participant's name was written on their forearm in Thai for easy reading, and hearing my name pronounced by the trainer with such accuracy revealed to me that Thai has a certain scientific structure to its phonetics.

Tucked away in the heart of Chiang Mai, a small boutique hotel offered a delicious Thai breakfast, spotless rooms with kitchenettes, and a washer and dryer available for nearly free. The staff was consistently gracious, friendly, and respectful. Oh, my Thailand—what a happy holiday!

Sis, Boom, Bar~

2024-03-16 (Sat)

How many people know what "Sis, Boom, Bar~" means? Likely, quite a few have heard it in passing. This was originally a rallying cheer from Princeton University in New Jersey, a prestigious institution vying with Harvard for the title of the top American university in the mid-to-late 19th century. "SIS" mimics the sound of a firecracker taking off, "BOOM" is the explosion, and "BAR" represents the cheer of people ignited by the display. In Korean, it might sound like "Piyung, Kwang, Woowa~."

Now, let's connect this to another memory. "Our Paichai School, Paichai School, let's sing, let's sing and sing again." This is a song familiar to many—the school song of Paichai School, Korea's second modern secondary school, founded in 1886 in Jeong-dong, Seoul, by Reverend Appenzeller, a Princeton graduate. The refrain, "Sis, Boom, Bar~," which Appenzeller adapted from Princeton's cheer, resonates with vibrant, thrilling energy even for those unfamiliar with its origin.

My older brother, who passed away about a decade ago and was ten years my senior, attended Paichai School long before I even started elementary school. As a young child who didn't yet understand the world, I remember him in his crisp khaki uniform, singing "Let's sing,

Paichai School, Paichai School" with his friends. Although I didn't understand much then, I can still recall the pride and camaraderie in their voices.

Reflecting on my family's history, Paichai School stands out as an unforgettable chapter. My father, who had worked as an elementary school teacher in Japan, returned to Busan at the age of 24 when Korea was liberated in 1945. As one of the few Koreans fluent in English, he soon took on a role managing military supply transportation for the U.S. military government, allowing him to live well for nearly 20 years. However, due to his gentlemanly, gentle nature that didn't suit the business world, his venture eventually failed. My parents then moved to a humble, thatched-roof house in the mountain village of Donam-dong, on the outskirts of Seoul.

During this time, my second eldest brother was a freshman at Paichai High School, in the throes of a sensitive adolescence. He couldn't cope with the shock of our family's sudden shift in fortunes and ran away to Busan, seeking refuge with his girlfriend. She was the daughter of a well-off family who lived in a grand, two-story western-style house in Bosu-dong. My mother, only 38 at the time, was so determined to keep my brother in school that she went there herself, bearing a rollcake as a bribery to school, carrying my then 2yr old yonger brother on her back by piggyback pleading for his readmission after he was nearly expelled.

Years later, through an incredible coincidence, I was contacted by no other than the younger sister of my brother's puppy love—the Bosu-dong sisters themselves. They had long since emigrated to Oakland, CA. Yet, somehow, after seeing my essay published in the Hankook Ilbo, aka The Korea Times America, they reached out, thrilled to connect with me in place of my late brother. That reunion felt nothing short of a miracle.

This reflection keeps the essence of your family's story, allowing an English-speaking reader to feel the emotional impact of your family's history and these cherished connections. Let me know if this captures what you were hoping for!

Paichai School has indeed produced many influential figures who have helped shape the Republic of Korea as it is today. Among them is Syngman Rhee, the first president, who is featured prominently in the documentary *National Foundation War,* a recent topic of great interest in the Korean film industry. Another significant alumnus is Park Dong-sun, a central figure in the 1976 Korea Gate scandal, a major event that left a lasting mark on modern Korean-American diplomacy. A 41 years old, Georgetown University graduate and chairman of Hannam Chain Market in New York, Park played a crucial role in shaping Korean-American relations, facing an investigation by the U.S. House of Representatives Ethics Committee on allegations of lobbying American politicians to support then-President Park Chung-hee. Remarkably, nearly 50 years after this pivotal event, Park is reportedly still alive at 88. I think of his contributions and the hardships he endured for Korea and wish him continued health.

Sis, Boom, Bar~ Paichai School!

Dedicated to the 40th Anniversary

Life of the SKY: The Family Magazine of the Air Force Alumni Association of Officer Candidate School - Commemorative Issue for Public Interest Corporation Designation

2024 3ʳᵈ month

Kim Duckhwan
78th Class Intelligence Officer/San Francisco

The initiation to military life in mid-March's chilly spring weather was daunting, with the stark reality settling in for 358 of us as we stood on the parade ground in front of the 78th Officer Candidate barracks at the Air Force Training Command in Tanbang-dong, Daejeon. Just the day before, we had officially entered the academy, and our admission was cemented through rigorous physical tests and exams.

Barely had we begun our first task—cleaning our combat boots—when we encountered the Instructor Officers' uncompromising attitude toward discipline. In less than three minutes, while hurriedly polishing with makeshift methods and spitting on the shoe to mix with wax to buff leather surface nose of the boots well, the Instructor Officers would march over, deliberately kicking our butts aside. Shouts of " What a slacker you guys are!" filled the air, leaving no doubt that our lives had taken on a new and rigid structure from that moment. It was a swift and decisive introduction to the discipline that defined our future as officer candidates.

I can still vividly recall Lieutenant Baek Seung-wook,

our senior platoon leader from the 29th Air Force Academy, tried to select the candidate of the loudest voice for an oath making person, and he gradually approached to me testing the voice of one by one , and I happened to be chosen as the loudest voice to make an oath at the ceremony. My heart pounded as he drew nearer, hoping I'd be spared, but, true to the nature of Murphy's Law, he singled me out. "You do it."

With adrenaline surging, I let out the loudest Pilseung! (means "Sure, victory!") I had ever managed to get applause and sighs of relief from my classmates, who were grateful to avoid the spotlight. This unexpected turn left me with the honor and nerve-racking responsibility of preparing for the entrance ceremony oath. For someone who had never experienced public recognition, the thought of freezing up and forgetting the words terrified me. Yet, somehow, amidst the greatest tension I'd ever felt, I delivered the oath smoothly. That marked the beginning of an unforgettable six-month journey that would shape us all.

Military training had begun. Those six months were undoubtedly the most pivotal, challenging, and proud moments of my life as an Air Force officer, which is as precious as Goryo Celadon. Reflecting back, the most strenuous sessions were undoubtedly the chemical, biological, and radiological gas chamber training, followed closely by individual combat exercises. We'd roll left and right across the "training ground" in the blistering heat, our mission to make it to the end—a task so grueling that I'd often end up losing the lunch I'd just eaten.

Despite my generally hearty appetite, the jjambbap, a military meal (slang) we'd line up for after those harsh training sessions was a culinary treasure. Soybean paste stew with fish cake in it, kimchi, stewed flounder, and even a carton of Seoul Milk—all of it felt like a feast beyond comparison. I would eat down to the very last grain of rice, which earned me the somewhat embarrassing nickname "Ssak-sri" (meaning someone who eats every last bit). Some of my peers even managed to sneak in an "extra round" at mealtime under the watchful eyes of our instructors—a bold feat I couldn't help but envy.

An unusual blend of pain, joy, and intense satisfaction marked those six months. Surprisingly, my biggest struggle was not the brutal combat or gas chamber drills but something as seemingly trivial as eating. After two months of grueling initial training, we were finally given our first snack: hardtack. I had looked forward to it for so long that I ate it too quickly, causing me to be sick. I couldn't even make it to the outdoor training ground in line without feeling faint.

In hindsight, the mix of exhaustion and fulfillment during that period left a deep imprint, guiding how cautiously I lived afterward.

I was in such a state of shock that I felt as if the sky would fall and I'd perish in mere minutes. There were no rapid-response systems like ambulances at the time, so I had to step out of the line, drenched in cold sweat, unsure of what to do. Thankfully, my colleagues had discovered that one of the Ha-hu, a fellow non-commissioned officer candidate training group, nearby, was a skilled in acupuncture.

He rushed over and swiftly applied two emergency needles he'd brought with him, and in that instant, I felt as if I was pulled back from the brink—a moment of sheer relief I'll never forget. To this day, I'm deeply grateful to that unnamed candidate who, with those needles, brought me back from what felt like certain doom. Wherever he may be, whether he pursued a career in oriental medicine or simply continues helping those around him with traditional remedies, I sincerely hope he's living a happy and fulfilling life.

Our officer training regimen was relentless. They claimed that, like African lions leave no traces, so we weren't allowed to sit down during breaks. Instead, we stood at attention in the blazing sun, soaking in each grueling moment. A particular highlight during training was when we heard the miraculous news through the loudspeakers: Coach Park Jong-hwan had led the Korean U-21 World Cup Soccer team to the semifinals of the World Cup—a feat that sparked immense joy among us. And who could forget candidate Shin Jin-yong, who serenaded us under the shade of a tree with "Sparrow and Scarecrow" during one rare moment of respite? Recognized by Samsung for his character and professionalism, he later built a successful career before founding his own mid-sized company.

Reflecting on my time in the Air Force, I can say without hesitation that those 42 months were among the most honorable of my life. I managed critical North Korean strike targets at the Osan Combat Air Command Intelligence Department, collaborating closely with senior pilots. I had the privilege of visiting Gunsan Air Base to observe the state-of-the-art F-16 squadron with US Airforce pilots—a mission steeped in significance as it followed special directives from then-President Chun Doo-hwan after the near-fatal Aung San Incident in Burma in 1983. I transferred to the Military Attaché Liaison Office, to take after the position of Captain Park Sung-hyun of the 75th class who was discharging from the force, liaising with various embassy attachés, which was an assignment I remain deeply proud of, even now in my early sixties.

Reflecting on 21 years in San Francisco, I've been fortunate to reconnect with old comrades of the Airforce, which made me feel happy and joyful in SF bay, though there are others I haven't been able to meet or support as I'd have wished. Sometimes, I regret that I couldn't assist my classmates' children as they settled here due to the demands of my own immigrant life, yet I trust they'd understand any small sadness I might feel about this. Meanwhile, I'm mindful of the eight vibrant friends who've left us all too soon, and it serves as a reminder of life's fragile, precious nature. Likewise, seeing friends persevere through unexpected health challenges fills me with hope and admiration.

To my cherished comrades, my wish is for all of us to stay healthy and content. May we come together in 10 years at the Air Force Hall in Daebang-dong to celebrate our 50th commissioning anniversary in strength and joy. Victory!

(California State Licensed Real Estate Broker / Palo Alto President of Galaxy Real Estate & Galaxy Real Estate School/ Korea Times America Headquarters Columnist)

Port Lee Arirang

2024-05-16 I)

Ah, the trials of travel! Spending the night on a cold airport floor at Las Vegas is a uniquely grueling experience. After a layover in Orlando, my Spirit Airlines flight at dawn left little time for rest. My makeshift arm pillow and trunk setup were a harsh reminder that age catches up with all of us, making those "innovative" sleeping positions much harder on the body. It felt like an unspoken rite of passage for seasoned travelers. I was finally on my way home to the San Francisco Bay Area after a 4-day, 5-night trip to New Jersey.

This trip marked my return to New York and New Jersey after almost 29 years. My last visit had been in January 1995, during a 45-day on-the-job training program hosted by MasterCard's headquarters in Manhattan while I was working for a major commercial bank in South Korea. Those memories came rushing back as I visited Fort Lee and Palisades Park, now buzzing with Korean culture—a marked shift from the days of Flushing. Upon my arrival, I met with a longtime elementary school friend, and we enjoyed a hearty dinner of Korean Army Stew at a local restaurant, accompanied by a bottle of makgeolli, a traditional rice wine and Pajeon, a green onion Pancake..

The experience left me astounded by the complexities of New Jersey's liquor laws. About $300,000 is the market price for a liquor license in New Jersey, which is a sharp contrast to California's straightforward application process, which costs only about $1,000 through the ABC State Department of Alcoholic Beverage Control. Surprisingly, despite these restrictions, customers could bring their own drinks from nearby convenience stores. "When in Rome..." I thought. Navigating the local rules felt like mastering an art form in itself.

Despite the exhausting journey, dinner with my friend provided a much-needed moment of comfort. Flying from San Jose to Newark wasn't the best decision, requiring several connecting flights and an arrival too late in the evening. A direct flight to JFK would have been much more practical and efficient. After dinner, I checked into the modest accommodations at Pal Park, or Palisades Park and tried to put my regrets behind me. Still, with the excitement of the reunion looming the next day at the nearby Hilton Hotel, I found myself staring at the ceiling, unable to sleep. I couldn't help but think about myself at younger times who used to fall asleep in a matter of minutes, no matter where he was, as if he could fall asleep on a pile of rocks. Now here I was, a weary traveler, counting sheep in vain, unable to rest.

The following day, alumni from as far as Vancouver, Toronto, Seattle, Cleveland, Washington D.C., and California gathered for our reunion. After a light meeting, some played golf, while others explored the city. Our group toured Manhattan's Fifth Avenue, visiting landmarks such as St. Patrick's Cathedral and the Summit One Vanderbilt—an impressive 101-story building with a glass observation deck, completed during the pandemic. We reminisced about our days at Myeongnyun-dong and Suwon Yuljeon campuses, where our passion for learning had driven us toward a brighter future. Hand in hand, we encouraged one another and strengthened the bonds of our alumni family.

Through their stories, I learned more about the Korean community in New York, many of whom arrived in the mid-1980s when there was a demand for pharmacists in the U.S. This influx of pharmacy graduates from Korea helped build a strong, supportive community. Now, those early immigrants—our steadfast silver-haired alumni—have settled down successfully, providing silent but powerful support to the group. Their enthusiasm and solidarity in this bustling city, the capital of the world, is unmatched. Whatever they do, they bring an unmatched energy that makes everything they touch incredibly "cool" and enjoyable.

After four days of reconnecting with these remarkable people, I returned home, sat at my desk, and sighed. Despite these meaningful reunions, I still haven't been able to track down my close friend and neighbor, Sungjin, a Vietnam War veteran from my days in Donam-dong over 50 years ago. Nor have I reconnected with Youngsu, a brilliant mind and Seoul National University graduate, whom I haven't heard from in nearly five years. Youngsu, how are you?

Epilogue

I am thrilled to share with my readers the joy of publishing a new book in the American market, marking a fresh chapter in my life. Two years ago in Korea, I published my first book, *Edelweiss, in San Francisco*. From the beginning, I dreamed of bringing my work to a global audience, republishing it on platforms like Amazon. Since that initial release, I've added 15 new episodes, including contributions to *The Korea Times America* and the Air Force Academy's *Life of the SKY* magazine. Now, with these additions, the book is reborn under the beautiful new title, *Winds From San Francisco: A Life Across Oceans*, and I can't describe the sense of happiness it has brought me.

I owe heartfelt thanks to Daniel and his assistant, Micahel from Authors Time, for their professional editing, design, and formatting work,

To the many readers who have embraced my essays, thank you sincerely. I hope to keep writing, to stay healthy, and to enjoy the company of inspiring people.

Finally, I would like to express my deepest gratitude to those who have been guiding lights on this journey: to my late father, Kim Man-jo, who passed away 45 years ago but left behind daily diary entries that pretty much inspired me to write well and with intention; to my younger brother, Seong-hee, who majored in creative writing at Chung-Ang University and surrounded me with good books that taught me about literature. Also, to my two elder sisters, whose remarkable memories of our childhood have enriched my own stories, and to all the wonderful people in my life who have, together, woven a tapestry of beautiful stories. Thank you for being part of my journey.

About the Author

Duckhwan Kim is a seasoned professional with extensive experience in corporate banking, insurance, and real estate. He graduated from Sungkyunkwan University, an institution within the SAMSUNG Foundation in South Korea, earning a Bachelor of Science in Business Administration and Management. Following his studies, he served as a First Lieutenant in the Republic of Korea Air Force for 42 months until August 1986.

In 2024, Kim became a distinguished listee of Marquis Who's Who recognized for his work ethic, patriotism, and positive impact on the community. Marquis Who's Who is a prestigious biographical reference chronicling influential individuals in the United States and worldwide since 1898.

With nearly two decades of experience in real estate, Kim is the founder and owner of Galaxy Realty and Finance, a respected firm in the San Francisco Bay Area. He also leads Galaxy Real Estate School, where he is dedicated to educating and mentoring aspiring real estate professionals. His school is widely recognized for its comprehensive curriculum and strong emphasis on preparing students for success in a competitive industry.

Beyond real estate, Kim is a regular columnist for the weekend essay section of The Korea Times America, where he shares insightful reflections on immigrant life, friendships, and the natural beauty of the San Francisco Bay Area. Through his work, he remains committed to supporting and enriching the lives of fellow immigrants as they navigate the challenges and triumphs of daily life.

About The Book

Winds From San Francisco:

A Life Across Oceans

By Duckhwan Kim

Transcending generations and continents, *Winds From San Francisco* is a heartfelt memoir intertwining stories of immigration, survival, and self-discovery. Duckhwan Kim recounts his journey from South Korea to America and reflects on the struggles and achievements of establishing a life in a foreign country.

With personal essays, Kim captures the elegance of cultural adaptation, the longing for home, and the bonds one forms along the way. From the hustle and bustle of Silicon Valley to the still corners of nostalgia, his rich storytelling presents a moving portrait of identity, friendship, and the chase for dreams.

With its humor and heart, Winds From San Francisco is more than a memoir—it's a tribute to the millions of immigrants who carry their heritage overseas and embrace new beginnings.